"After seeing the Cirque du Soleil creative team in action, up close, during the making of *Toruk*, I often said that Hollywood could learn a lot from the Cirque culture of putting creativity first, before all other considerations, at every step of their process. I was truly inspired watching them work, and this book will provide important insights about how that ethos is balanced against the demands of business and the real world."

—James Cameron,
Filmmaker

"In contemplating the last fifteen years of partnership between Cirque Du Soleil and The Beatles' Apple Corps, I've realized that this relationship is the ultimate example of creativity, collaboration, and perseverance. It has been a 'long and winding road,' and at every turn *LOVE* has brought joy, inspiration, storytelling, and exhilaration to audiences who come to be enveloped and transported by the iconic music and the multisensory motion of the show. So many creative, caring, and passionate professionals, both at Apple Corps and Cirque du Soleil, are responsible for nurturing what began as magical musings between George Harrison and Guy Laliberté. Working with Daniel has been a journey that has enlightened and enriched me, both personally and professionally, and for that I am forever grateful."

—Jeff Jones,
CEO of Apple Corps

"With a wholly unique creative spirit, Daniel Lamarre has established himself as a visionary leader by growing Cirque du Soleil into a globally beloved brand and redefining modern live entertainment in the process. Now, through this book, he's using the same singular sense of imagination that made Cirque du Soleil's *Joyà* such a smash hit at Vidanta Riviera Maya to illuminate the importance of bringing creativity to every aspect of your life."

—Daniel Chávez,
Founder of Grupo Vidanta

"The relationship between MGM Resorts and Cirque du Soleil is synonymous with Las Vegas's evolution as the Entertainment Capital of the World. From the first tent show behind The Mirage in the early 1990s to the four incredibly successful shows currently running on the Strip, we have created a destination unlike any other in the world. I've been honored to work alongside Daniel Lamarre for twenty years during both good times and challenging ones for our organizations. His book is a great reminder that creativity and business should not be treated as two separate entities. When working together symbiotically, they have the ability to drive an organization to even greater heights."

—Bill Hornbuckle,
President and CEO, MGM Resorts Group

"Cirque du Soleil has a well-deserved reputation for extraordinary creativity and the unsurpassed quality of its shows, and we are proud and excited to be partnering with them in bringing one-of-a-kind entertainment to guests of all ages."

—Bob Chapek,
President and CEO, The Walt Disney Company

BALANCING
ACTS

Unleashing the Power of Creativity in Your Life and Work

DANIEL LAMARRE

EXECUTIVE VICE CHAIRMAN, CIRQUE DU SOLEIL

With Paul Keegan

HarperCollins
Leadership

AN IMPRINT OF HarperCollins

Published by HarperCollins Leadership, an imprint of
HarperCollins Focus LLC.

Any internet addresses, phone numbers, or company or product
information printed in this book are offered as a resource and
are not intended in any way to be or to imply an endorsement by
HarperCollins Leadership, nor does HarperCollins Leadership
vouch for the existence, content, or services of these sites, phone
numbers, companies, or products beyond the life of this book.

ISBN 978-1-4002-2303-9 (eBook)
ISBN 978-1-4002-2302-2 (HC)

Library of Congress Control Number: 2021948888

Printed in the United States of America
22 23 24 25 26 LSC 10 9 8 7 6 5 4 3 2 1

It is with great emotion
that I dedicate this book to two amazing women:

To my mom,
for supporting me all my life.

To my wife, Emmanuelle,
for being part of this great adventure.

CONTENTS

——

Dear Reader,

Why, you may be wondering, should you read a book by a businessman whose company had to file for bankruptcy protection?

It's a question I welcome because it gets at the heart of what I want to convey about the power of creativity.

Let me explain. By early 2020, my fourteenth year as chief executive of Cirque du Soleil, we had grown into a global entertainment powerhouse with forty-four live productions around the world. Annual revenue had soared to $1 billion, our brand was a beloved household name, and I had begun writing this book about the indispensable role of creativity in building a great company.

Then the COVID-19 pandemic struck. As the deadly virus spread across the planet, we had no choice but to shut down all forty-four shows and seek court protection from our creditors. Tragically, I had to lay off 95 percent of our five thousand employees as our revenue dropped to zero. My book was in limbo. After all, who wants to read about a company at death's door?

And yet, I was determined to not only save Cirque but also continue writing about what I was learning. That's what kept me going. Then, in our darkest hours, something miraculous happened: I began fielding calls from blue-chip investors hoping to buy us out. Even *I* was stunned. How could a company with no sales, a skeleton staff, and no timetable for resuming operations become the object of a bidding war?

The answer was soon clear: investors were attracted by the tremendous power of our brand and the value of our intellectual property. Within a few months, we were acquired by our creditors, a group of financiers who absorbed our $900 million debt and invested an additional $375 million to bring Cirque back to life. That put the market value of our company, even in a crippled state, at a stunning $1.275 billion.

This improbable sequence of events illustrates why creativity is so vital in business—better than anything else I could say in this book. After all, we have no physical products, no factories or inventory, no pricey real estate. Instead, we have something far more valuable: the limitless creativity that springs from the minds, hearts, and bodies of our artists.

In fact, I would argue that whether you are an entrepreneur, an executive, or a professional, if you are not prioritizing creativity—in the dictionary definition of "making or bringing into existence something new"—you are wasting your time. No company deserves to exist unless it is constantly discovering new ways to make its customers' lives better. In short, without creativity, there *is* no business.

For most people, the gargantuan challenge of our time has been COVID-19. But any unforeseen event, at any time, can knock your company, or your career, off balance: a new technological development, a competitor's product launch, a natural disaster, an economic crisis. As you'll see in these pages, no matter the source of your troubles, creativity is the key to help you surf those waves and thrive again.

Today, I'm happy to say, Cirque du Soleil is back. Our resident shows in China and Mexico were the first to return, followed by our iconic Las Vegas productions *Mystère* and *O*, then *Michael Jackson ONE*, *The Beatles LOVE*, and *KÀ*. Tickets sold out quickly, and restless audiences poured back into our theaters, ecstatic to see live entertainment once again. As we continue to relaunch shows in other parts of the globe, the astonishing feats on our stages remind the world that anything is possible.

I feel privileged to have guided Cirque du Soleil for the past decade and a half and deeply proud of our resilient artists. I hope you'll find the lessons in this book helpful and that you'll come away profoundly inspired to bring forth great wellsprings of creativity into your personal and professional life.

Sincerely,
Daniel Lamarre

INTRODUCTION:
WITHOUT CREATIVITY, THERE
IS NO BUSINESS

———

As the audience settles in the darkened theater, acrobats playing Liverpool sailors climb ropes dangling from the ceiling and the lush a cappella harmonies of Paul McCartney, John Lennon, and George Harrison fill the air.

It's June 30, 2006, opening night of *The Beatles LOVE* at the Mirage in Las Vegas. At the time serving as the chief executive officer of Cirque du Soleil, I'm a bundle of nervous excitement. I can't just relax and watch the show like everybody else. Instead, my mind races back to the long series of improbable events that led to this magical moment: our first meeting with Paul, George, Ringo, Olivia Harrison, and Yoko Ono in a London hotel suite; the endless negotiations with so many parties—the Beatles' management firm, Apple Corps; the record companies; the Mirage owner, MGM Resorts International—before finally getting the deal done; asking the "Fifth Beatle," George Martin, and his son Giles to create the soundtrack; watching Paul appear at dress rehearsals to encourage our awestruck cast and crew.

Looking around at the inspired design of *The Beatles LOVE* theater reminds me of another major turning point that illustrates one of the most difficult challenges to living a creative life: how to bridge the gap between a brilliant idea and its practical execution.

———

Two years earlier, as president and chief operating officer, I had the unenviable job of convincing the Mirage to blow past its $30 million budget for renovating this theater. Our designer, Jean Rabasse, and his team wanted to get rid of the traditional proscenium structure (with the audience facing the front of the stage) and replace it with a theater-in-the-round concept with tiered seating. Spectators, looking down at the stage, would feel like they are inside a big-top tent; the design would also subtly evoke the Beatles' famous 1969 rooftop concert in London. The plan included placing sixty-three hundred speakers throughout the theater—including small units built into the front and back of every seat—to make the remix by George and Giles Martin sound as magnificent as possible.

There was one big problem with this beautiful vision. MGM had just spent huge sums to build the massive moving-platform stage for *KÀ*, our spectacular new show at the MGM Grand, and was in no mood to break the bank again. A renovation budget of $30 million may sound like a lot, but that's really only the bare minimum for all the complex rigging and technology our resident shows require.

Seeing a major clash in the making between our design team and MGM's budget constraints, I knew I had to act—quickly. I had only been at Cirque for a few years by then but had come to understand a fundamental truth about the symbiotic relationship between money and creativity: they both desperately need each other.

Armed with detailed renderings of the proposed theater design, I flew to Las Vegas with Cirque cofounder Gilles Ste-Croix to make our pitch directly to Bobby Baldwin, chief executive of MGM's Mirage Resorts subsidiary. Bobby already had a full schedule on his calendar, but this couldn't wait. So Gilles and I decided to surprise him at his regular table in his favorite restaurant.

"What are you doing here?" Bobby demanded when we approached. "I'm having lunch!"

"We just need five minutes of your time," I said, pulling out the renderings and outlining the concept. "Look at that—isn't that an amazing theater? Wouldn't it be perfect for a Beatles show?"

Bobby shook his head. "You know the budget," he said. "I can't do that for $30 million."

"But it's gorgeous!" Gilles said. "It's just what we need for an amazing show to bring in huge crowds!" Those crowds, he didn't need to add, would spend heavily at the Mirage on hotel rooms, shopping, food, drink, and gambling. That's our usual deal with resorts that host our shows: they build the theater, and we bring the crowds.

Soon our five minutes were up, but we made sure to leave our renderings on the table.

A few days later, Bobby set up a video conference with our entire creative team. "Daniel," he said from the screen as the meeting began. "How much do you think it will cost to build the theater you're asking for?"

I shrugged. "I know nothing about construction costs in Las Vegas—"

"Well, let me tell you," he said. "Your fucking theater will cost $90 million!"

At the conference table, we all looked at each other, wide-eyed. Triple the original budget!

"Yes, well, that *is* quite a lot," I said. "Did you call this meeting just to tell us that?"

"No," he snapped. "I called the meeting to be on the record with all you creative people sitting around that table: this had better be a goddamn great show!"

The room erupted in laughter. At that early stage in the process, nobody knew what kind of show we would create or how successful it might be. But Bobby clearly had faith in us. He was willing to make a $60 million bet that Cirque would once again accomplish what we had done for other MGM properties with *Mystère* and *O*: produce a show that would sell out for years to come, spreading joy and wonder to legions of fans and making millions for both of us.

Until that moment, however, not everyone at Cirque was sure I truly understood why our productions were so wildly successful: we had established a company culture that prizes creativity above all else. As a newcomer, I still had much to prove. Was I the type of executive who would throw up his hands and say, "Sorry, folks, MGM just doesn't have the budget for this"? Or would I fight hard for them?

Now they had their answer. As the meeting ended in smiles and laughter, I could feel that the creative side looked at me differently. Trust had been established. They saw that I would not hesitate to leverage all of Cirque's clout to convince a prominent Vegas executive to spend an extra $60 million so they could make the show of their dreams.

And what a dream it was. Back at the Mirage, the Beatles are singing the final gorgeous harmonies of "Because" from *Abbey Road*. The sailors slide back down their ropes, and the final chord of "A Day in the Life" rings out (played backward), followed by the opening chord of "A Hard Day's Night." In the next moment, Ringo's drum solo from "The End" fully ignites the show, the stage exploding with light, sound, and color as dancers in flamboyant costumes let loose. We hear the sound of fans shrieking, wailing guitars, and Paul's voice blasting through state-of-the-art speakers: "Jojo was a man who thought he was a loner, but he knew it couldn't last. . . ."

By now, the audience is hooked. The theater's design has brought us so close to the action that we feel like we're *in* the show as well as part of a close community of fans surrounding the stage on all sides. Such an immersive experience would have been impossible in a traditional theater. And audiences know they're getting something special. Except for a seventeen-month hiatus during the COVID-19 pandemic, *The Beatles LOVE* has run continuously for more than fifteen years.

Eventually, the cost of renovations climbed to $100 million. Suffice to say, the Mirage made its investment back—and then some.

THE POWER OF CREATIVITY

To be creative is to make yourself vulnerable. It's human nature to hesitate to let our ideas and emotions flow with the kind of abandon necessary for true innovation unless we feel we can trust the people around us. That's why it's so important, in any creative endeavor, to establish a safe harbor.

For the last two decades, that's been my job at Cirque du Soleil: establishing the conditions for creativity to flower. I've always loved being around artists of all kinds, though I never was one myself. I was a conventional businessman in my midforties when I joined this inspiring, astonishing, wacky circus in 2001 as a senior executive. That's when I discovered my mission in life: to create jobs for artists. For me, there is no greater joy than to give the green light to a new show because it triggers the hiring of another brilliant director, creative team, and dozens of cast and crew members.

At Cirque, I learned not only about creativity—what it is, how it operates—but also about its incredible power. When I first arrived at our headquarters in Montreal, the consensus within the company was that we had saturated the market with our seven shows—two resident productions in Las Vegas, one in Orlando, and four on tour—and the only way to grow was to diversify into other businesses, from themed resorts to nightclubs. That makes me chuckle now. Creativity was so deeply embedded into our DNA that our artists couldn't help but dream big, launching new shows, one after another, with audacious concepts—the moving stage of *KÀ* from acclaimed director Robert LePage; *The Beatles LOVE*; *Toruk—The First Flight*, based on James Cameron's *Avatar*, and much more. Each time, we took bigger and bigger risks. Rather than cruise on what we had accomplished or allow changing trends and tastes to render us outdated, we entered a phenomenal period of expansion. Over the next two decades, we grew more than sixfold to forty-four shows (including acquisitions), with annual revenues doubling from $500 million to $1 billion.

By early 2020, we had seven resident shows in Las Vegas alone; one each in Orlando, China, Germany, and Mexico; and thirteen touring productions that covered enormous swaths of the globe. In all, our touring shows had reached 450 cities in sixty countries including all of Europe, most of South America, Japan, South Korea, Saudi Arabia, Dubai, Israel, and New Zealand. More than 200 million spectators have seen a Cirque show since the company's founding, and our fifteen million ticket buyers in 2019 were more than those of all thirty-nine Broadway shows combined. Our staff more than tripled to five thousand employees (hailing from forty-nine nations). Operating profit margin reached 20 percent (EBITDA), and we still had almost limitless potential in the largely untapped markets of China, India, and Africa.

That kind of growth was only possible because we were never satisfied with the status quo. Over the years, our productions have evolved into a completely original art form with elements of circus, drama, comedy, dance, performance art, live musical concerts, and high-tech stagecraft, accessible in any language or culture. That, combined with our mastery of the complex task of touring the world with our massive shows, makes us impossible to copy and protects our market share. Our customer-loyalty index (known as "Net Promoter Score") is as high as Apple's, and we consistently rank among the most unique brand names on the market. After we expanded further by acquiring smaller entertainment companies like the Blue Man Group, VStar (with kids' shows like *PAW Patrol* and *Trolls*), and The Works (The Illusionists magic show), our goal broadened: we wanted to become nothing less than the biggest and greatest live-entertainment company in the world.

THE WORLD STOPS

We all know what happened next. When the COVID-19 pandemic hit in March 2020, our lives were turned upside down. We had to immediately close all forty-four productions around the world. Revenue dropped to zero. In, by far, the most painful moment of my career, I had no choice but to lay off 95 percent of our five thousand workers.

Just imagining the shock and financial stress our employees would have to endure was heartbreaking. But as the pandemic wore on, I became fueled by the flip side of that awful situation—an intense drive to save the company and rehire those artists. With COVID-19 out of control, we had no shortage of critics predicting our demise. But anyone who has seen a Cirque du Soleil show knows that we traffic in the impossible. And sure enough, we came roaring back.

I will tell the whole astonishing story in chapter 7. For now, it's enough to note that the same force that gave birth to Cirque in the mid-1980s—a passionate, relentless drive to create—is what saved us during one of the worst global crises of the past century.

"BRING INTO EXISTENCE SOMETHING NEW"

In my travels, I am often asked to give speeches to explain how Cirque du Soleil, after nearly four decades, has remained so boldly creative while also enjoying such tremendous commercial success. Those two qualities, after all, are often considered mutually exclusive. My answer comes in a mantra that anyone eager to thrive in a dynamic, rapidly changing global economy should take to heart:

Without creativity, there *is* no business.

I mean that quite literally. And I'm not talking only about the entertainment industry. A few years ago, Cirque du Soleil cofounded, along with advertising executive Jean-François Bouchard, a conference devoted to creativity and commerce called C2 Montréal. Every year, it attracts thousands of participants from all over the world. As I listened to the challenges and successes of entrepreneurs, executives, and employees from every type of firm, in a wide variety of industries, I became more and more convinced that we have reached a critical turning point: Today, after decades of advanced technologies and the exponential growth of social media, nurturing a creative work-place is no longer an option. It's an absolute necessity.

At one C2M panel, a bright young lawyer asked me why her company should worry about being creative. I get this kind of question all the time, usually from people who think their industry is too conventional to make innovation a top priority. "Just consider how drastically your job is changing," I told her, list-ing the many ways content distribution is redefining the whole notion of intellectual property and how social media is changing the meaning of laws created only a few years ago when paper and landline phones were the primary means of communication. There is nothing more important in her job than foreseeing and adapting to these dramatic changes, but the challenge is even greater than that. She and her firm must realize that incremen-tal steps are not enough. They must completely reimagine their business from the bottom up, expanding the boundaries of what is possible. People who can do that, in every business, will be the winners in tomorrow's economy. Those who can't will soon be obsolete.

I use the word *creativity* a lot, so I should probably explain what I mean by the term. My favorite definition comes from the *Encyclopedia Britannica*: "the ability to make or otherwise bring into existence something new, whether a new solution to a prob-lem, a new method or device, or a new artistic object or form."

I like that formulation because it's both simple and wide-ranging, allowing any company or industry to see why creativity should be a central part of its mission. What could be more important than discovering new ways to help your cus-tomer or client?

The specific method each firm or individual uses to priori-tize innovation will vary widely, of course, but here's an idea of where to start: I often ask executives outside of the entertainment industry what percentage of their resources—from budgets to employee hours to C-suite attention—are devoted to coming up with new ideas or solutions to the challenges their companies face. Usually, the answer is "Not much." I can relate. That's how I would have answered the question in my pre-Cirque days. Now, with the zealousness of a convert, I can testify from experience that when a company devotes significant attention and resources to creativity—consistently going where few dare to tread—it's astounding what can flourish.

When anyone asks me what keeps me up at night, I usually say, "Imagining someone else at the top of our industry." That would mean Cirque had lost its leadership position. To prevent that (and help me get a good night's sleep), we decided to make a serious commitment to research and development. We hired three full-time employees to do nothing but search the world for new ideas and talent in all cultural sectors: music, fashion, architecture, theater, film, games, and more. Meanwhile, our research department, C-Lab, hunts for innovations in areas like science, technology, and biology that are ready for practical application. When you go to a Cirque show and see something spectacular that you have never seen before, or even heard of, chances are good that it came from one of these initiatives.

One important aspect of establishing a creative culture is being able to respond quickly to changes on the ground. The world moves so fast today that you must be able to improvise like a jazz musician. In a live-entertainment company like ours, anything can go wrong at any time. A cast member gets sick or injured. Backstage technology malfunctions. Our creative team decides a show needs a new direction. Weather events disrupt a touring production halfway around the world. A natural disaster, public health emergency, or trade war breaks out, interrupting our expansion plans.

We are not unique in that respect. Today, every company must be able to operate with a sense of urgency. Here's a question to ask yourself: Does your entrenched bureaucracy allow you to react quickly and calmly when something goes wrong? When your computer system is hacked, a supplier goes bankrupt, a competing product is unexpectedly released, or the economy tanks? As the world becomes more interconnected and technology accelerates the pace of change, agility is critical. If you're busy filling out forms and studying your next move, chances are your competitor has already beaten you to the punch.

THE AGE OF THE ARTIST

When I lay out these arguments, a common reaction is, "Well, it's easy for a successful company like Cirque to make creativity a high priority. But how can the rest of us afford it?" I would turn this logic around: putting creativity first is precisely *how* Cirque grew from a tiny circus troupe into a global powerhouse. Yes, having patient owners willing to invest gave us considerable resources to take risks. But, like any other business, we have budgets and deadlines to meet, not to mention the mind-boggling logistical challenge of transporting our shows around the world (up to seventy trucks of equipment for big-top touring shows). We could never have reached our level of achievement without being extremely practical and mindful of the bottom line. And that creates a virtuous circle: creativity makes us profitable, and those profits allow us to be creative.

This is truer today than ever before. At age sixty-eight, I can look back and see how profoundly today's business landscape has changed since I started out in the 1970s. Consider what the tech revolution alone has wrought. With the world's aggregated knowledge just a click away and core business functions increasingly done by robots, having a particular expertise or skill set is not nearly enough. Today, workers must possess qualities that machines are not capable of—precisely the sort that artists spend their lives developing: imagination, spontaneity, nonlinear thinking, openness, discipline, empathy, compassion, and more.

This shift is so pronounced that I am convinced that we are on the precipice of an entirely new era. Call it The Age of the Artist. The evidence is all around us. According to the McKinsey Global Institute, the jobs most resistant to automation are those that rely on "soft skills" like managing and developing people, decision-making, planning, creative work, and interacting with customers and suppliers. Another study from Harvard found that nearly all job growth over the past thirty years has been in such "social skill–intensive" areas. Entrepreneurs and the self-employed are affected too. As consumers flock to niche products and the internet lowers the barriers of entry for starting a business, an artisan economy has flourished, allowing creative people to build sustainable careers.

It's ironic that working and thinking like an artist, once seen as a path to poverty, is becoming a powerful way to get ahead—and a smart way to manage millennials, who increasingly demand a strong sense of purpose in their work.

Today, there is often a disconnect between younger employees and more senior managers who have trouble motivating employees who expect more than a paycheck from their jobs. Thinking in terms of creativity can help. Though Cirque is fortunate to have world-class performers already passionate about what they do, we have some of the same employee engagement challenges as other companies. The further our people are from the stage, we have found, the harder it becomes to inspire them. Our solution is to make *everyone* feel part of our exciting shows, whether they are working in finance, information technology, or human resources. Managers in any company can do the same by making all employees feel they are a vital part of whatever is the most fascinating, glamorous, or socially beneficial part of their firm's mission.

For me, the best part of speaking at C2 Montréal and other events is hearing back from audience members who face these issues and send emails that say, "Can I meet with you to ask for some advice?" As often as I can, I say yes because I love that feeling of helping someone. And I think we've all had the experience of listening to a speaker and realizing, *Hey, I've been struggling with this problem for weeks and this person just helped me click on a solution.*

That's why I am writing this book. I want to use my experience at Cirque to help people foster creativity in their organizations in ways that increase their profitability. Over the years, I have seen a tremendous yearning for guidance on this topic—from executives and managers, entrepreneurs, professionals, students, fans of our shows, and people with creative ambitions from all walks of life. I have become convinced that human ingenuity is a huge, untapped resource that most companies are not anywhere near taking full advantage of.

My hope is that this book will resonate deeply regardless of what industry you are in, from so-called creative fields like film, media, or architecture to more conventional industries like construction, health care, manufacturing, and finance. To those who don't think of themselves—or their jobs—as being especially artistic, I have a secret to reveal: creativity is for *everyone*. When nurtured with care, it can bring you to a whole new level of accomplishment.

To be as useful as possible, each chapter will be sprinkled with practical advice illustrated with real-life examples of Cirque's challenges, triumphs, and failures. Chapters will, for the most part, progress chronologically to allow readers to see how these principles helped transform the company from a small street troupe into a global phenomenon, all told from my perspective as a conventional businessman who gradually comes to understand and find his place in Cirque's singular culture.

Along the way, I will pull back the curtains for a rare inside look at how our iconic shows were created. I will discuss how we handled, and sometimes bungled, crises like the financial meltdown of 2008, the flop of our vaudeville show *Banana Shpeel*, the raging tsunami that hit Japan while we were performing there, and, of course, the devastation of the COVID-19 pandemic. Though we have an unusual business—your colleagues may not wear extravagant costumes and fling themselves through the air on a regular basis—I think you will find that many of the issues we face are not much different than your own.

Most of all, I hope this book serves as an inspiration and guide as you work through your own challenges, in business and in life.

May the light of creativity be your North Star.

Let the show begin!

CHAPTER 1

FROM A SMALL TOWN TO TRAVELING THE WORLD

My life—and my whole approach to business—changed forever one morning in November 2000, when I received a phone call.

"Daniel, how are you?"

It was Guy Laliberté, the founder of Cirque du Soleil.

"I'm doing great," I said. And truly I was, having been CEO of one of Canada's largest television networks for the past four years and enjoying it immensely.

"No, no, you can do better!" said Guy, practically screaming into the phone. The big conglomerate that had recently bought my company would make my life awful—*miserable*, he shouted. "You have to get out right away!"

"Whoa, whoa, whoa," I said. That's classic Guy ("Ghee," as we Québécois pronounce it)—impulsive, funny, dramatic, and, at this moment, rather confusing. "What are you talking about?"

"I had this amazing flash last night," he said. "You are going to join the circus!"

I laughed, unsure of what to say. "Listen, I just want to know," he went on. "Are you at least open to discussing it?"

I had a thousand reasons to say no. First, I barely knew Guy. We had some interactions when my television network, the TVA

Group, bought the rights to broadcast Cirque shows. And years before, my public-relations firm had done a short job for him. Like most people in Quebec, I knew Guy was an eccentric musician and fire-breather who started Cirque du Soleil in the mid-1980s with a ragtag group of street performers in Montreal. But that was about it.

Plus, his timing was terrible. At forty-seven, I was in the prime of my career in the media business, making a good salary with plenty of stock options. I had just bought a beautiful house on a lake outside of Montreal. Why would I jeopardize all that?

And yet, something told me to meet with Guy and hear him out.

Three weeks later, I joined the circus.

I am not, by nature, a risk-taker. Growing up poor in the small industrial town of Grand-Mère, Quebec, had made me determined to never have to worry about money the way my parents did. So, after graduating from Ottawa University, getting married, and having two children, I gave up my plan to be a newspaper reporter and settled into a safer, more lucrative career in public relations, advertising, and later, television. Since my college days acting in a theater troupe, I've always loved being around artists. But in my career, I never imagined being anything other than a successful, conventional businessman.

Then along came Guy, inviting me to become Cirque's president of New Ventures with a path to eventually succeed him as chief executive. As I thought about his offer, everyone close to me said I was crazy to even consider it. Cirque was a much smaller company then, still trying to prove itself and only a bad show or two from folding its tents for good.

But I was surprised to find, stirring within me, a long-dormant craving for adventure. I had always been intrigued by how Cirque created its astonishing shows, especially *O*, the Las Vegas hit that converted the Bellagio Hotel and Casino stage into a huge water tank. How on earth did they turn such wild ideas into a profitable, growing business? I could sense that this move—in addition to costing me plenty of stock options—would force me out of my comfort zone and into a brand-new world of possibility, a prospect I found both electrifying and terrifying. Wracked with indecision, I put Guy off as long as I could until I finally shocked even myself by blurting out, "Yes, yes! Let's do this!"

A few weeks later, as I walked into company headquarters in Montreal—where all Cirque productions are dreamed up and rehearsed—I had no idea what I was in for. Nobody does, since no background can prepare you for this carnival fun house, with acrobats flying through the air in cavernous studios and bustling workshops filled with mannequins decked out in outrageous costumes. All I could do, I realized, was explore this peculiar place, try to fit in, and hope for the best.

My entry shock was immediate. When I arrived for the press conference announcing my appointment, Yasmine Khalil, then in our marketing department, took one look at my suit and tie and said, "No, no, no, you can't go out there looking like that! Nobody wears a tie at Cirque du Soleil!"

Guy was not there—he would be appearing via video from London—and that was a good thing. Whenever a suit like me showed up at headquarters wearing a tie, he would grab a pair of scissors and gleefully snip it off. (He always said he planned to make a Hawaiian lei out of the hundreds of fragments he collected.)

FIND YOUR PASSIONATE CORE

It was my first lesson in Cirque's unusual approach to business management: the biggest priority is to have fun. Without a spirited approach to life, the company's stage miracles would be impossible. Later, Guy was worried that I was *still* being too serious, so he assigned me my own personal clown. Her name was Madame Zazou, and she would follow me around, keeping me and other employees in stitches. She would barge into meetings, unannounced, and say, "Aren't you tired of listening to these boring guys?! Come on, stand up!!" Then she'd lead everybody in a ridiculous exercise class while singing silly songs she made up about whatever show we were working on. By the time she left, everybody was feeling loose, connected, and inspired.

Whenever I tell this story to a business audience, I stress that it should be seen strictly as a metaphor. Obviously, you are not going to hire a clown because that's not your business. The important point is to ask, "What would be the equivalent for *my* company?" Madame Zazou taught me that every firm can find creative ways to remind employees of their mission. Finding the passionate core of your company is a critical first step in discovering what those inspiring symbols and rituals might be.

Back at the press conference, Yasmine was not nearly as destructive toward my wardrobe as Guy would have been, but she was no less direct: she yanked off my tie, pulled off my suit coat, and handed me a Cirque du Soleil jacket. When my old boss at TVA, André Chagnon, saw the press conference on television later, he almost didn't recognize me. "What's next, Daniel?" he said. "Are you going to start wearing an earring? Maybe a ponytail?"

André was teasing, of course, but I got the point. Maybe taking this job was a big mistake. In my first year, I tried hard—and often failed—to fit in. I was hired for my experience, but my experience kept getting in the way. Several times I wanted to quit. But I hung in there, got tremendous support from Guy, and eventually found my place, working my way up to chief executive nearly six years later, in 2006. Along the way, I had to change the way I think, the way I talk, even the way I dress—a transformation as complete as that of any cast member who puts on the makeup and costumes of our shows. I did not start wearing an earring or grow a ponytail, but I did show up at work in jeans, boots, a casual shirt, blue-tinted glasses, sometimes a colorful ascot. I was surprised to find that adapting to the artistic culture of Cirque, even in small ways, made me more relaxed and productive.

Looking back, it's funny how my reputation within the company changed. For a long time, I was considered The Boring Businessman while Guy was The Brilliant Artist. We both knew that was an exaggeration—Guy has a shrewd business mind and I've always had a passion for the arts. Yet those images persisted. So when Guy decided to sell most of his majority stake in 2015 for a reported $1.5 billion, employees became terribly nervous, afraid that he would not be around to stop our new owners— the private equity firm TPG Capital—from ruining the fertile artistic culture that made Cirque so special.

Fortunately, that never happened. From day one, I told the executives at TPG, "You can come into my office ten times a day if you want, and I'll give you all the financial and operational information you need. But don't *ever* go into the creative department. They have to be left alone to work their magic."

Drawing that line in the sand made everyone relax. Backstage after a show, cast members would rush up to give me big hugs. At that moment, I knew my conversion into a creative executive was complete.

TAKE CARE OF ONE ANOTHER

Looking back, I am amazed that I ended up running a circus company. After all, the global stages of Cirque du Soleil are a long way from my hometown of Grand-Mère. And yet I've been surprised to discover how crucial small-town values are for nurturing creativity and achieving success, not just at Cirque, but in the wider business world as well.

When I was a child, my four siblings and I never felt poor. But we definitely were. When I was six years old, my younger brother and I went to the barbershop and asked the barbers to just cut *some* of our hair because we only had fifty cents between us. The men laughed, escorted us to our chairs, and gave us the full treatment.

It was an early lesson in generosity and loyalty that I never forgot. Today, many people associate capitalism with selfishness and greed—and understandably so. But when I consider what techniques have worked best for me over the years, I think back to my formative years when citizens of our blue-collar community were always taking care of one another, never hesitating to pitch in when times were tough.

My family wholeheartedly embraced that way of life. When my father became ill with a digestive condition, he spent a year in the hospital, and our family's financial condition worsened. He was not strong enough to return to his job at a local textile factory, so he decided to change his life in a big way, transforming himself into an office worker to support our family. My dad went back to school, got a job at a bank, and eventually worked his way up to become bank manager, president of the local chamber of commerce, and a respected leader in our town.

It was so inspiring to watch my father climb the ladder. I remember thinking, *If he can get that far, maybe I can do something with my life too!* Even more impressive was that he never left the less fortunate behind. Even as he struggled to establish himself in a new field, he found the time and energy to raise money for a summer camp for underprivileged children, Camp Lac-en-Coeur ("Lake of Heart"). He truly wanted to help those kids, never expecting that the connections he made among wealthy and powerful benefactors would help his career—and yet they certainly did. (Today it gives me great pleasure to raise money for the very same charity, which named a new building after my father.)

Though my dad was always an inspiration, it wasn't until I got to Cirque that I understood how the lessons he taught me about community applied to the creative process. Forget the myth of the lone genius changing the world through his or her grand vision. Creativity is a team sport. Just look at Paul McCartney and John Lennon, who needed each other to produce their beautiful music. Or Steve Jobs and Steve Wozniak, neither of whom could have founded Apple Inc. alone. If you look closely enough, you'll see that the key to extended success for any creative team lies in a strong sense of allegiance to one another. That's really the glue that holds everything together.

BUILD RELATIONSHIPS BASED ON LOYALTY

I got a big lesson in the power of loyalty many years later, in my first interactions with Guy Laliberté. It was 1986, when I was a senior partner at National Public Relations in Montreal. Guy showed up at our door looking for help to bring his exciting new circus troupe, then just two years old, to the next level of success.

Though I had never met Guy before, I knew all about Cirque du Soleil. Everybody in Quebec did, ever since it burst onto the scene during the 1984 celebrations of the 450th anniversary of French explorer Jacques Cartier's voyage to Canada. In those early days, Cirque was still a nonprofit and struggling financially. Guy was hoping my firm could help him attract sponsors and donors from the business world and lobby the government for more arts funding. It was a short job, lasting only a month or two, and when it was over, I presented Guy with our invoice for $25,000.

What I didn't realize was that during this brief period, Cirque's finances had gone from bad to worse. Later, I found out that it was nearly bankrupt. When he got the invoice, Guy came to my office and said he was very sorry, but his company simply did not have enough money to pay it.

At that moment, I suppose I could have yelled, demanded immediate payment, and threatened to sue. That never occurred to me. As a Québécois, I was so proud of what Cirque had accomplished, and I wanted to support our local artists any way I could. So I tore up the invoice and dropped it in the wastebasket. "Guy, what you are trying to do is so fantastic," I said. "I wish you the best of luck."

It wasn't until a decade later that I realized how powerful that moment would turn out to be. By the late 1990s, Cirque had become a thriving international brand and I had moved on to the TVA Group television network, a big player in the world of Canadian media. In my role as chief executive officer, I became interested in obtaining the rights to broadcast Cirque shows. When I called Guy, he said he already had a deal with an international television distributor. "I understand," I said, and we hung up after a friendly exchange.

Neither of us had mentioned the torn-up invoice, but the very next day, I was copied on a note from Guy to his marketing vice president. "This guy helped me years ago," he wrote. "He wants our TV rights, so do whatever you have to do."

I was surprised and grateful that Guy had remembered. Eventually, he got the rights back from the distributor and made a deal with us. During the three years that we worked together, Guy and I got to know each other a little better. The final payoff came when he called out of the blue to offer me the job at Cirque that changed my life.

When I tell this story, people often say it was kind of me to forgive Guy's debt. I don't look at it that way. Don't get me wrong. Kindness is an important quality to me, as it should be for any leader. But with my Grand-Mère upbringing, it was simply second nature to show loyalty to a member of our community—in this case, a trailblazing artist who was putting on such amazing shows.

Loyalty, for me, is another way of saying "thinking long term." A short-term strategy of suing Guy would have forced me to expend so much negative energy, in time and resources, that it would have likely been a losing battle for both of us. Being loyal, on the other hand, meant thinking about the future and the promising relationship that could develop. I never dreamed that forgiving that debt would boomerang back in such a powerful way, of course. I simply liked the idea of a rising star like Guy Laliberté thinking well of me.

This approach has its limits, of course. Had the bill been for millions of dollars, and had I felt that my firm was **being** mistreated or exploited, I would have done what I had to do to protect the company. I'm certainly not naive. But if the short-term loss is minimal, and there is good faith on both sides, I try to avoid conflict and litigation whenever possible. Some would say that's being soft. I say it's being smart.

This has always been my philosophy, but it was nice to learn that research backs me up. In his writings, business psychology expert and Wharton School professor Adam Grant provides a mountain of evidence that people he calls "givers" often end up being more successful than "takers." Givers who can avoid becoming pushovers or doormats, he found, ultimately find that their good deeds come back to them in spades. This has been my experience as well. Think of it as karma, corporate style.

I found it interesting that Grant concludes that givers are not necessarily altruistic because they understand that qualities like generosity and loyalty may benefit them down the road. Their distinguishing feature is that they look for gains that do not come at the expense of others and remain ready to pay their success back and forward, even when there appears to be no immediate benefit from doing so. This creates what Grant calls "a ripple effect, enhancing the success of people around them."

Takers, on the other hand, try to get more out of each relationship than they give and want to win at every turn, regardless of how it impacts others. That route to success often breeds envy and resentment as people look for ways to take these people down a notch or two. All actions have consequences, of course, but the path of givers ends up being far more productive in the long run. "It's easier to win," the venture capitalist Randy Komisar says, "if everybody wants you to win."

In retrospect, I can see how my simple act of tearing up that invoice resonated with Guy, a deeply loyal man. At the time, I had no idea. It took several years, once I joined Cirque, to get to know Guy well enough to fully understand his values and absorb the story of the troupe's early days. That helped me to better understand the culture and the principles embedded in its DNA, how those beliefs were surprisingly much like my own, and how my own traditional career path led, improbably, to a gut-level decision to join the circus.

REINVENT YOUR INDUSTRY

My research into Cirque led to some elaborate case studies by academics trying to pinpoint the sources of our company's success. In 2004, for example, the business-school professors W. Chan Kim and Renée Mauborgne celebrated Cirque as a model for creating and dominating new markets in their best seller *Blue Ocean Strategy*.

When that book came out, Guy and everyone else at Cirque were proud to be considered innovators who could inspire other firms to discover their own "Blue Ocean" markets (the opposite of overcrowded "Red Oceans," stained by the blood of competition). But it also seemed quite funny that distinguished professors would climb down from their ivory tower long enough to study techniques that Guy and his motley crew of stilt-walkers, fire-breathers, and clowns had learned on streets—or simply made up as they went along.

The founders of Cirque were essentially a group of hippies who wanted to reinvent the world—and much of the company's success has flowed from that basic impulse. This was not a business strategy. They just wanted to have fun, travel the world, and challenge conventional notions of reality. Every new entrepreneur would do well to remember just how essential that kind of passion is. Given the huge obstacles, starting a successful new business is almost impossible without a single-minded devotion to shaking up the established order.

Much of Cirque's spirit can be traced back to the cultural upheaval of the 1960s, which included a vibrant street-performer scene. Two of the company's early influences—Gilles Ste-Croix and Guy Caron—were artists active in the network of communes and cooperatives that flourished in Quebec. By the mid-1970s, Caron was producing shows and exhibitions at a Montreal café and took under his wing a teenage musician named Guy Laliberté.

Laliberté was a precocious lad whose gifts as a producer were apparent even in high school, when he organized a school trip to Cajun Louisiana from scratch—raising funds, getting permission from parents and the school, and arranging the travel. He also loved performing, playing accordion and singing in a folk group that toured the Quebec festival circuit. After high school, he headed for Europe, sleeping on park benches and meeting acrobats, mimes, and other street performers from whom he learned skills like walking on stilts and breathing fire.

At the age of twenty, Guy met Gilles Ste-Croix, who was managing a youth hostel near Quebec City. Gilles agreed to give the young man food and lodging in exchange for providing entertainment on the premises. The older artist, who would later become one of Cirque's top producers, had a tremendous impact on Guy. "He's the father of Cirque," Gilles likes to say. "I'm the grandfather."

The roots of what became Cirque du Soleil began with a theater troupe Gilles founded called Les Échassiers de Baie-Saint-Paul ("The Stilt-Walkers of Baie-Saint-Paul"). In the summer of 1982, the group created a weeklong festival with

Guy as general manager. Though it lost $10,000, it made that money back and then some the following two summers. Guy was demonstrating his knack for balancing creativity with the bottom line and began thinking about establishing his own company. "If we put all this under a big top and toured with it, we'd have a circus," he reasoned. But what to call it? On a trip to Hawaii, he was on a beach watching the setting sun—*soleil* in French—when the name occurred to him. "The sun stands for energy and youth," he said, "which is what I thought the circus should be about."

Through his festival work, Guy made a connection with Jacques Renaud, director of programming for Quebec's mammoth celebration of Jacques Cartier's historic voyage to Canada. He saw his opening. Guy teamed up with Robert Lagueux, a trumpet player and arts marketer, to create a proposal for a touring show they called Le Grand Tour du Cirque du Soleil. An acquaintance of Guy's from high school, Daniel Gauthier, came on to handle administration and finances. Eventually, the group received $1.6 million in government funding to tour eleven towns over thirteen weeks in the summer of 1984.

It's not hyperbole to say that Cirque's debut marked the beginning of a revolution in the circus arts. Until then, the only circus most Québécois had ever seen was the traditional Barnum & Bailey, on tour from the United States. Creatively speaking, the circus industry was old and tired, a relic from another era. Guy and his collaborators wanted Canada to have its own national circus with a highly theatrical, character-driven narrative, original music, flamboyant costumes, and no performing animals to distract from the human story. I remember going to some of those early shows as a young man and being stunned by how different it was than any production I had ever seen.

After securing government funding for another year, Guy hired as artistic director his old friend Guy Caron, who had gone on to create the National Circus School in Montreal. They brought aboard another visionary, Franco Dragone, who would have a huge impact on the company. A teacher at Caron's circus school who specialized in acting and commedia dell'arte, Dragone would later direct every Cirque show during a remarkable period of success in the 1990s.

"To me, the big secret of Cirque du Soleil is that we created shows like a film," Caron says. "We thought it should be edited and scored like a film. If you take the music out, you don't have a Cirque du Soleil show. Cirque is like cinema: you edit it together to create drama, and to allow people to enter completely into the experience, like you do into a film screen. You enter into the experience and forget anything else."

As Cirque's distinctive brand was being developed, the company had trouble making its shows resonate beyond Quebec. That's a common challenge for any company trying something new; at first, people might not understand what the heck you're doing. As the troupe ventured to Ottawa, Toronto, and Niagara Falls, crowds became increasingly thin. By the end of 1985, Cirque was a whopping $750,000 in debt. I've often wondered whether I would have taken them as a client at NPR around this time had I known how much red ink they were bleeding.

But Guy and his crew hung in there, limping along with government grants until they reached a major turning point in 1987. A new production, *Le Cirque Réinventé*, was their most ambitious yet. Inspired by the Parisian show *Paris-Peking*, it told the story of ordinary people accidentally stumbling into a magic circus and being transformed into performers and acrobats. Generating considerable buzz, the show soon attracted the attention

of Thomas Schumacher, associate director of the Los Angeles
Festival, who came to Montreal to scout it. He was blown away.
"What we saw was what everyone in Montreal and Quebec had
been seeing for years, which was complete magic because you
climbed inside this yellow-and-blue tent and it exploded out,"
Schumacher said later. "It was as if it was bigger than anything
the tent could contain."

There was a snag, however. The festival could not afford the
huge cost of bringing the show to Los Angeles, nor could it pay
the performers. Guy had a big decision to make. Transporting
the cast, crew, and truckloads of equipment all the way from
Montreal to Southern California would consume all of Cirque's
limited resources. Guy negotiated the best deal he could with the
festival producers: securing the opening slot, promises of heavy
promotion, and a guarantee of 100 percent of ticket sales. But
if the show were a flop, the company would literally not have
enough money to return home. And that would likely mean the
end of Cirque du Soleil.

Any company trying to create a market where none has ever
existed faces such an existential dilemma at some point. Inevitably, there comes a time when you must either forge ahead—
hoping your instincts are right and your research is thorough—or
pull the plug and go do something else. After coming this far,
Guy was not about to turn back. "I'm not going to wait twenty
years to see if we can make a living off what we do," he con-
cluded. "The opportunity is here; let's make a deal."

On to Los Angeles they went. On opening night in September of 1987, Guy's relentless networking had succeeded in
packing the room with celebrities like Sylvester Stallone, Arnold
Schwarzenegger, and executives from Columbia Pictures. The
pressure was intense, but the performers rose to the challenge.

The show was an instant hit, and tickets suddenly became a hot commodity. The *Los Angeles Times* said the performance "obeys our prime command as a circus audience: Astonish me. It also obeys our hidden command: Scare me. There's a moment when a female high-wire artist seems to lose control, 60 feet up in the air, and, oh, God, you can't look. But you do."

Finally, Cirque du Soleil was not merely an artistic success, but a commercial one too. Profits in Los Angeles fueled its push into Las Vegas, Europe, Japan, and beyond. The hippies from Montreal who wanted to reinvent the world had succeeded beyond their wildest dreams. By essentially creating a new art form, Cirque not only established an unexplored market but pioneered an entirely new business model based on a single imperative that would become mandatory for survival in the twenty-first century: the restless need to create.

EMBRACE THE DRAMA OF LIFE

As Cirque's early history shows, the company operated in crisis mode from day one. I wish I could say that things get easier as your firm gets bigger and more established, but it's not true. No matter your size, thriving in today's hyperconnected global economy means being in a constant state of alert and ready for anything. In our case, with dozens of productions around the world, we know that some catastrophe is always lurking that calls for quick and decisive action.

Since avoiding the sudden twists and turns of life is not an option, the best approach is to embrace them. Fortunately, I have always been drawn to the excitement and challenge of dramatic situations. That's why I originally wanted to be a journalist. The summer of my sixteenth year, I had a job at a fast-food place selling hamburgers and french fries and hated it. When I told my dad I wanted to quit, he challenged me to figure out what I *really* wanted to do. One night, lying in bed, I wondered how I could tie together my interests in areas like sports, theater, and politics. Suddenly, an idea popped into my head. I got up, found my parents at the kitchen table, and said, "Dad, I want to be a journalist."

Taking me at my word, the next day he got me a job at our local weekly newspaper. Getting paid to ask questions, learn about the world, and meet important people was heaven, and I was soon hired by a big regional daily. Even in college at Ottawa University, majoring in communications, I worked side jobs as a reporter. But journalism wasn't the only place to find drama and excitement. I also played on the college football team and joined the theater company (perfect training for Cirque's culture of athletes and artists!). In the end, I was not temperamentally suited to be an actor, especially because of the emotional strip-tease one must perform, but I never lost my love of theater and respect for artists.

After graduating, getting married, and starting a family, I gave up my journalism career. I was tired of covering other people's lives and wanted to be a player myself. Plus, being a reporter seemed like an unstable profession. So I took jobs in public relations and advertising—a compromise that I thought would allow me to be creative but still have a stable, if somewhat boring, career.

Creative it certainly was. As it turns out, I didn't have to worry about the boring part.

DEAL WITH CRISES HEAD-ON

I'm quite sure I could not have done my job as CEO of Cirque—flying around the world putting out one fire or another—without some critical lessons in crisis management during my career in public relations. The most important of these lessons sounds simple but can be difficult to execute: you must face crises head-on, without the evasions, delays, and cover-ups that companies often engage in. Understand that, and you will thrive in today's chaotic world. If you don't, you may not survive the next crisis (which will probably come sooner than you think).

I learned this lesson soon after my first big career break, when the largest PR firm in the world, Burson-Marsteller, approached me through a headhunter and hired me to open its new office in Montreal. I was twenty-eight years old and overwhelmed by the sheer size of my new employer, with offices all over the globe. Suddenly, I realized there were vast opportunities in international markets, which proved to be great training for Cirque. So was creating special events—like promotional campaigns at car races for a beer company—which was like putting on shows.

My work soon drew the attention of someone who would become an important mentor, the great Harold Burson himself. One of the most influential figures in modern public relations, Harold was a trusted adviser to the heads of some of the biggest corporations on the planet. And in my second year with the company, he gave me an invaluable primer in how to deal with a crisis. In September of 1982, everybody at Burson-Marsteller was shocked when one of our clients, Johnson & Johnson, was rocked by the now-famous Tylenol poisoning tragedy: seven people in the Chicago area died after taking capsules laced with cyanide. Though I didn't work directly with Harold on this account, I followed his work closely and watched the drama unfold in real time. I was impressed when he advised James Burke, the CEO of Johnson & Johnson, to be completely transparent with the public and immediately recall 31 million bottles of Tylenol from store shelves.

The short-term hit for Tylenol was tremendous, of course, costing the company more than $100 million. But with public safety at stake, there was no room for half measures, compromises, or corporate spin. Facing the crisis directly, it turned out, actually helped the bottom line in the long run. Most analysts predicted the company's reputation would never recover, but Tylenol's market share rebounded within a year. It was an inspiring performance for Harold, who had a gift for making clients see that focusing exclusively on their own short-term interest, at the expense of others, is ultimately self-defeating— especially during a dire emergency that demands a broader view.

A few years later, I had the chance to put what I learned into practice in a very similar situation. In 1984, after three years at Burson-Marsteller, I left to become senior partner at National Public Relations. It was not an easy decision—there was substantial risk because I would be part owner of the company— but I could not pass up the chance to work with founder Luc Beauregard, another man of great vision and integrity. It turned out to be a great boost for my career: together, we turned Luc's small organization of just twenty employees into the largest public-relations firm in Canada (ironically, eventually acquiring Burson-Marsteller's Canadian operations).

Not long after I started my new job, I was in my car, heading for an important meeting, when I got a call from André Tranchemontagne, president and CEO of one of our biggest clients, Molson Brewery.

"Can you come to my office right away?" he asked.

"Well, I'm on my way to a very important meeting," I said. "But as soon I'm through—"

"No, you don't understand!" he interrupted. "I need to see you right away!"

I canceled my meeting and headed straight to André's office, where I found him surrounded by his senior management team. "A caustic and potentially lethal substance was found in our beer," he explained. "We believe it may have been caused by a mechanical failure on our assembly line, but we have not found the exact source yet."

André fixed me directly with his gaze. "Since you went through the Tylenol crisis, I want you to help us decide how to proceed to protect our company."

In the room, the atmosphere was thick with tension. I began sharing the lessons I had learned from Harold Burson, the same ones I use in whatever crises I face today:

- *There must be only one decision-maker.* "And that's you, André," I explained, making it clear to everyone in the room who would be calling the shots. When there is a crisis, everybody wants to get involved, and everybody wants to be celebrated as the savior of the company. You must not allow that. Do not operate by committee and waste a lot of time debating and agonizing because there is no time to waste: decisions must be made quickly and implemented even faster.

- *You must learn the magnitude of the crisis.* Investigate the causes of the problem and calculate how many people are affected. Do this quickly and get your facts right. If you don't understand exactly what you're dealing with, you'll never be able to solve the problem.

- *Short-term financial considerations should not come into play in your decision-making.* The stakes are far too high. Your challenge is nothing less than saving the brand, possibly even the company itself. Focus only on being transparent and fixing the problem. This can be the hardest step because people in the company will try to hide the facts, cover their butts, and minimize the impact. That only makes the problem worse, possibly making it spiral out of control.

I was fortunate that André listened to everything I said with an open mind and accepted my suggestions on the spot. He did not shirk responsibility, assumed a decisive leadership role, and confronted the issue directly with a dramatic public announcement: the Molson plant had been contaminated, and all bottles would be recalled from store shelves at once.

There was an immediate uproar. The media was full of stories about consumers suffering burns from the toxic bottles, and pundits predicted the company's demise. Despite the panic inside and outside the company, André remained calm. After two days of testing, the source of the problem was found: leaks were causing toxic chemicals to poison the beer. After taking another full day to repair the equipment, we organized a press conference to share the good news. Surprisingly, that only served to inflame the situation as the media used the opportunity to sensationalize the story even further.

Molson's final challenge was to retrieve all the existing bottles from the market. That was quite complicated because thousands of cases were located in the most remote parts of Canada. When that job was finally complete, the company was ready to announce that there was no longer any danger to consumers. But many people on André's leadership team felt that holding a press conference would only rile up the press again, giving it more ammunition to attack us. I took the opposite position, arguing passionately that sending the company president in front of the cameras was the only way to assure the public that we were not trying to hide anything. Fortunately, I was able to turn to Alban Asselin, Molson's public affairs vice president, to join me in the fight for transparency.

For hours, we debated the issue. The meeting lasted until 9:00 p.m., and the cumulative fatigue of the last few days was palpable. Our discussions were increasingly emotional. Finally, André made his decision. "We have been transparent with the media since the beginning of the crisis," he said gravely. "We must conclude on the same note." He instructed me to arrange a press conference for the day after tomorrow, a Friday.

At the end of that very long day, I sat in my car, exhausted. Checking my voicemail, I found two messages. The first was from Francis Armstrong, my partner at National Public Relations, who had an idea: to celebrate the end of the crisis, he suggested an advertisement offering a free beer to all consumers. *What a ridiculous idea*, I thought, too tired to even consider it. The second message was from my then wife, Josette. When I called her back, she sounded irritated. "Where *were* you?" she demanded. "What do you mean?" I shot back. "You know I've been spending my days at Molson, managing the crisis."

There was a pause, and Josette laughed. "I think you're the only one who thinks there's still a crisis," she said. "It hasn't even been mentioned in the media for two days."

IT'S NEVER TOO LATE TO MAKE
A CREATIVE DECISION

I was stunned. Could it be true? Immediately, I realized that André's executives had been right: if we went ahead with the press conference, we would stir up the media's thirst for sensationalism all over again, and nobody would pay attention to the good news. I had been so wrapped up in the emergency that I hadn't noticed that the rest of the world had moved on.

It took all the courage I possessed to call André back and explain that holding the press conference would be a serious mistake. He was furious, and I could hardly blame him. "Daniel, you spent the whole day defending the opposite position," he thundered. "What's the matter with you?"

Unable to convince him over the phone, I made an appointment for dawn the next morning at his office. I asked my colleague Francis to join me because suddenly his idea of giving away beer to celebrate the end of the crisis didn't seem so ridiculous after all. After much discussion, we won André over. Instead of holding a press conference, we issued a press release explaining our wacky promotion.

It was a brilliant stroke: all the subsequent press coverage focused on the cleverness of our advertising campaign. The toxic leak was quickly forgotten, and, on Saturday morning, when consumers throughout Quebec saw the full-page ad in their newspapers—"Free Beer!"—they flocked to stores to claim their bottles of Molson. Within a month, the company had increased its market share and later received several awards for managing the crisis so well.

Within that single episode were many lessons. Strictly speaking, Molson did not need to give away so much beer, at a cost of millions. But its generosity went a long way toward rebuilding goodwill with consumers, the company's way of saying, "Forgive us, and please stay with us." The incident also taught me how important the perspective of outsiders is to the creative process. Moments of crisis require innovative thinking, something that can be hard to come by when you are lost among the trees, unable to see the forest. Those two phone calls from people with a fresh way of seeing things—Francis and Josette—made all the difference.

Finally, the story offers insight to people who say, "At my company, we don't have the time to be creative, especially during a crisis, when there is barely a moment to think, let alone devise some ingenious new plan." But creativity is more about fostering an environment that allows ideas to flower. The "free beer" idea came to Francis in a flash, showing that it's never too late to make a creative decision that can save the day.

PRIORITIZE CREATIVE RISK

With potential disasters constantly looming like storm clouds, one might think the best strategy is to go through life with extreme caution, taking every measure possible to mitigate risk. As counterintuitive as this may sound, I have found exactly the opposite to be true. Risk is so central to the creative process that trying to eliminate it can kill the spirit of freedom that lies at the heart of true innovation.

In fact, I would argue that insulating yourself from danger is the biggest gamble of all because it can keep you stuck in a rut, leading to stagnation and decline. That spells big trouble in a world where competitors are always innovating and searching for signs of weakness, ready to pounce.

These principles apply even when managing your career. When I left National Public Relations in 1997 to become president and CEO of the TVA Group, the move was a huge gamble: my mid-six-figure income, plus bonuses, was instantly cut in half. Because TVA was a publicly traded company, my salary was published, and my former partner at NPR, Luc Beauregard, saw it. "Daniel, I thought you were crazy," he called to tell me. "Now I *know* you're crazy."

Of course, being smart about risk means ensuring there's a strong upside if you succeed. In the case of TVA, my bet paid off when the stock options I negotiated increased sharply in value, more than making up for my pay cut. But the reality is that I wasn't thinking much about money when I took the job. Mostly, I was excited about moving into the world of television and the rare chance to turn this small local network into an international force. People inside and outside the company literally laughed when I revealed plans to produce shows to sell around the world. But that's exactly what we did, growing to become Canada's leading French-language network.

The move paid off in another important way by preparing me for my job at Cirque. At TVA, for the first time, I had to manage the creative process by working with artists, directors, and show creators. I had to stay within program budgets and manage the sensitivities of actors and writers. I learned how to limit my involvement to an overseeing role—not interfering with the day-to-day work of developing TV shows—and making sure our broader goals were being met while inspiring and challenging our artists.

Considering that I was seen as the dull businessman when I arrived at Cirque, it's funny to remember that, at my television and PR jobs, I was known as the super-creative one. At NPR, I was always coming up with crazy, out-of-the-box ideas to promote Molson beer or a banking client. At TVA, I thought of myself as having a great artistic sensibility. How little I knew. Today, after two decades at Cirque, it's almost painful to realize how conservative I had been, how much further I could have gone, and how many opportunities were lost.

In those days, television had a very traditional mindset. Now I can see how blind we were to the digital future that would soon arrive with streaming services like Netflix. We were trapped in a conventional business model of creating prime-time shows and selling advertising rather than experimenting with new trends like viewing-on-demand and subscription services. We also didn't go nearly far enough in creating content for the growing international market.

Over the years, I have noticed that many managers don't make creativity a priority because they think their job is to tell people what they *can't* do. At TVA, we were afraid to take chances on anything that might risk a ratings drop. If I went back to that job today, I would earmark a portion of our budget for crazy ideas—nothing that would put the firm at risk, mind you, but one or two shows per year with the potential to become huge hits.

Just think about a show like *Seinfeld*, which many TV executives rejected because it was about a small group of single people in New York City with eccentric personalities who find themselves in bizarre situations that poke fun at social customs and dating rituals. But after years of low ratings, it became one of the most popular sitcoms of all time. Today I would tell my most ambitious creatives, "Come at me with your wildest ideas!" To have a true breakthrough, you must feel free to break the rules. And I should have reached beyond the world of television professionals to find inspiring artists in live-entertainment fields like comedy, music festivals, and theater who would challenge my industry's stale assumptions and preconceptions.

Anytime you take creative risks, of course, you get pushback. Shareholders and factions within the company will look at the portion of your budget being earmarked for generating new ideas and see a chance to save money and boost profits. They will argue that the chances of that investment paying off are remote. The key is how you defend that spending, appealing to the listener's intelligence by explaining your logic. You can't just say, "We're going to try something crazy!" Rather, you must explain the potential payback down the road. But what if six months goes by without a breakthrough? One year, two years, three years? In that case, retooling the projects in question may be required, but you must be extremely specific in outlining proposed changes and explaining why they will eventually lead to success. Over time, if you still can't justify a project, perhaps it deserves to die.

Prioritizing creativity, whether in business or life, often means being ready to fight for your ideas. Too frequently, I see people say, "Oh, nobody will support me," or "My bosses are too conventional; they won't accept this." That way of thinking sets you up for failure. A better approach is to say, "I'm dealing with intelligent people who can understand what I am trying to achieve."

The truth is, nobody can read your mind. You must explain in detail what you are doing and, if a project is floundering, how you will improve the situation. If your listeners can follow your rationale, chances are they will understand and support you. And, you'll find, one spectacular success will make everyone forget your misses.

RUN AWAY WITH THE CIRCUS

In this chapter, I have discussed key principles such as loyalty, reinvention, honesty in times of crisis, and creative risk. There is one more I would like to cover because all the preparation in the world won't amount to much unless, at some point, you're ready to run away with the circus.

Obviously, I am not expecting you to literally join a traveling entertainment troupe. In the public imagination, the idea of joining the circus exists mostly in the realm of myth, a metaphorical shorthand for doing something wild and adventurous. That's really what I am advocating here. In life and business, it's far too easy to become complacent. Sometimes real growth only happens when we dare to make the bravest leap of our lives.

My biggest professional risk was joining Cirque, but that may not have happened at all without inspiration from an amazing Olympic athlete named Sylvie Fréchette. Sylvie was the pride of Canada, not only for winning a gold medal in solo synchronized swimming at the 1992 Olympic Games in Barcelona, but for accomplishing that feat in the wake of an unimaginable tragedy. Shockingly, her fiancé died by suicide a week before the Games opened.

At the time, I was still at National Public Relations and Sylvie was my client. After she won the gold, it was not hard for me to line up an extremely lucrative job for her as spokeswoman for a large bank. The work was not difficult, and she would never again have to worry about money. I felt I was doing a great job, and I was happy she was once again thriving.

Then one day Sylvie showed up at my office with a video of Esther Williams, the competitive swimmer who made the leap to Hollywood in the 1940s and '50s with a series of hit musicals featuring extravagant aquatic numbers. "I don't want to work for a bank," Sylvie said. "That's not who I am. All my life, I've always dreamed of doing big shows like Esther Williams. That's what I want to do now."

"Sylvie, Sylvie," I said, shaking my head. "Those kinds of shows don't exist anymore. Those movies were made a long time ago. Be happy with your bank gig. It's the best job in the world. You're financially set for life."

She left, unhappily, and called me sometime later, bursting with excitement. "Have you read this morning's paper? Guy Laliberté is going to do a water show in Las Vegas. I want to be in that show!"

"Don't do this to yourself," I said. "It's a crazy idea. Keep your safe job at the bank."

But Sylvie insisted with the same indomitable will that made her an Olympic champion. So I had little choice but to contact Cirque, all the while telling her that she was making a huge mistake. That was my first contact with some of the amazing people at my future employer, colleagues like Lyn Heward and Gilles Ste-Croix, with whom I would later forge such tight bonds of friendship and professional and artistic respect.

Sylvie was perfect for *O*, the water show, but I soon learned that my usual approach of negotiating a contract for a big star would not work in this case. At Cirque, there is a saying, "The *show* is the star," which means that artists must leave their egos at the door and commit to being part of an ensemble.

As Sylvie's manager, I told her that not getting star billing was yet another reason why she should not do this—along with a vastly reduced paycheck. But she was determined. Sylvie was bored at the bank, craved being in a creative environment, and had no doubt that she was doing the right thing.

By the time *O* opened in 1998, I had left my public-relations job and had joined TVA Group. I will never forget the day I was sitting in my office, with its multiple television screens flashing away, and glanced up to see an arresting image: Sylvie was sitting by the pool on the set of *O*, smiling next to an elderly woman. I turned up the sound, and the announcer said the woman with Sylvie was none other than seventy-seven-year-old Esther Williams.

I couldn't believe it. I was so happy for Sylvie, who had made her dream come true after so much struggle and heartbreak. Tears began streaming down my face. *Daniel,* I said to myself, *everything you thought was wrong for Sylvie was actually so very right.*

At that moment, something changed in me. At the time, I couldn't say exactly what it was. But I would find out later when Guy called to offer me the job at Cirque. I had always dabbled in creative projects at various jobs. But I was still basically a rather ordinary business executive whose main responsibilities were bureaucratic. Talking to Guy about joining his crazy circus made me realize that my own creative impulses had been, for far too long, tamped down by the need to fit into the conventional structures of my positions.

This was my chance to do what Sylvie had done. I thought she was so brave to abandon the security of her bank job to literally dive into the pool at *O*. Now was my opportunity to do the same, metaphorically speaking. It was time to take my own risky dive into the unknown.

CHAPTER 2

DISCOVERING THE CREATIVITY
BEHIND THE CURTAIN

When I told my parents I was going to work for Cirque du Soleil, they thought I had lost my mind. "Oh my God, what is he *doing*?" my mom told my dad. After enduring years of poverty, they had been so proud as their eldest son rose to a prestigious job running a big television network. Now I was throwing all that away to join a circus? And what about my new boss, this ex-fire-breather Guy Laliberté, who seemed a bit peculiar? "You're sure you want to work with this guy?" my dad said.

Josette also thought I was making a mistake, the natural concern of a spouse learning that Cirque could not match the stock options I was getting at TVA. But I have never been motivated by money. When you're passionate about what you do, I have found, the financial end of things tends to take care of itself. Still, I didn't want to be stupid in making this move. I told Guy he would have to match my salary and offer an incentive package to eventually make up for those lost stock options. He did, and when Cirque took off in the 2000s, the deal paid off. But, at the time, it was quite risky. Many thought Cirque had no more room to grow, and, in a fickle and rapidly changing entertainment market, its fortunes could easily spiral downward. I knew I could be making the biggest mistake of my life.

For three weeks, I agonized over whether to take the job. The title would be president and chief operating officer of New Ventures, a newly created position to help Guy achieve his dream of diversifying into areas like real estate. If I succeeded, he planned to groom me to one day replace him as CEO.

All that was very appealing, but most convincing was Guy saying, "I read in the paper that you want to work internationally. It will take years to get there at your TV network. At Cirque, you can do it tomorrow morning if you want to."

LISTEN TO YOUR INTUITION

Hearing that was very exciting. I had always wanted to play on the global stage, and this was my chance. When it came time to give Guy an answer, something inside me said, *This is an adventure you* have *to take*. In a way I could not explain, my whole career seemed to be leading up to this moment, from my first interactions with Guy to seeking out creative jobs in public relations and television to my epiphany watching Sylvie Fréchette taking that leap to live out her dreams. It was quite a lesson: At every moment in your life, follow your intuition. You never know where it might eventually lead.

This gets at something I often tell people who come to me for career advice: think about how your job (even if you're not crazy about it) can become a springboard for your next act. What are your passions? Stay true to what motivates you, and always be on the lookout for ways to express it. That can result in some unexpected and hugely satisfying outcomes.

BUILD A CREATIVE ENVIRONMENT

It was in early December of 2000, after the press conference announcing my appointment, that I got my first tour of Cirque's headquarters, built three years earlier. Before that, the company was scattered across more than a dozen studios in Montreal, which became more awkward and inefficient as it grew. That led to Guy's grand vision for a central location to house the entire operation: a "creative hub" where all the shows could be developed and athletes and artists could train; a place where new employees could live in dormitories upon arriving from all over the world; a place where costumes could be sewn and music composed, where corporate offices could be built so all employees, no matter their role, could stay close to the creative process.

Guy found a spot in the Saint-Michel neighborhood of Montreal, about thirty minutes from downtown. Built on a former landfill, the massive 400,000-square-foot complex helped to revitalize a poor and neglected neighborhood and beautified the area with its shrubs, apple trees, and rose bushes. A garden produces vegetables and herbs for meals prepared in the company kitchen and served in the cafeteria, where employees relax, socialize, and brainstorm. Eventually, approximately one-third of Cirque's employees would be based at the headquarters, the rest divided about equally between our touring and permanent shows.

As I toured the complex for the first time, my head was spinning. I felt like Philemon, the boy in *O* who is plucked from his seat in the audience and tossed into a strange and wonderful fantasy world. The company's creative spirit is palpable at every turn—from a sculpture by the famed Quebec artist Jordi Bonet to a wall studded with colorful pieces of costume fabric to the

"Alley of Clowns," with photographs of Cirque's most memorable clowns. Young athletes walk around in tracksuits talking animatedly in different languages—Chinese, Russian, Spanish, German, you name it—making the place feel more like a vibrant college campus than a corporation.

I visited the dance and music studios, the gymnasium, and the three acrobatic studios, including the main rehearsal space: at sixty feet high and well over fifteen hundred square feet, it's large enough to stage an entire big-top show. Upstairs in the conference rooms (each one named after a Cirque show), windows overlook the studios, giving our executives a distinct edge during business negotiations. We make sure to sit with our backs to the windows so visitors sitting across from us are constantly distracted—and amazed—by the sight of trapeze artists soaring through the air while music plays and acrobats spin and twirl on trampolines.

In our costume shop that occupies two floors, a massive "fabric library" contains thousands of swatches for designers to select from as they create our stunning costumes. Workers are bent over three hundred sewing machines on the second floor, producing everything a show requires, from garments to hats and headgear to custom-made shoes. In the makeup studio, artists are trained to apply their own makeup (with up to sixty performers in each show, there simply isn't time for makeup artists to do it all).

No matter where you are in Cirque's headquarters, it's impossible to forget the company's artistic mission, articulated in large lettering on the wall: "*Invoke* the imagination, *provoke* the senses, and *evoke* the emotions of people around the world." That could also be defined as its social mission. When rehearsing any production, there could easily be more than a dozen languages spoken. What better model for global harmony than watching artists from all over the world bridging the divides of language and custom and culture—even those from nations that are sworn enemies—to put together a spectacular show?

My tour was a revelation: to be truly creative, you need a creative environment, one that encourages innovation even in the smallest informal exchanges between employees. I was impressed by how many meetings were taking place, in the corridors and the cafeteria as people lingered over lunch. Or they unexpectedly ran into each other and soon found themselves in deep conversation about the projects they were working on. That's something you don't often see in traditional companies. It seemed more like a place of higher learning, where people were constantly talking, debating, dreaming, sketching, writing, stretching, singing, dancing. Inspiration can happen anytime, when you least expect it. Having a physical space that encourages random, serendipitous encounters seems about as close as you can get to an ideal work environment.

Companies in other industries should build their creative environments to suit their mission, of course. The offices of the pet-supply firm Bark in New York and Columbus, Ohio, for example, make it impossible to forget the firm's purpose: more than two hundred fifty office dogs wander the halls, and next to each desk are side seats made of easy-to-wipe fabrics so the dogs can sit next to their masters. In Billund, Denmark, Lego's child-centric approach is evident everywhere you turn, from the playrooms that stimulate workers' imagination to whimsical touches like a curving tubular slide instead of stairs. Whatever your field, walking through your facility should make you *feel* the creativity underlying your core business.

SOMETIMES, IGNORANCE IS BLISS

Inspired by the tour, I finished up my work at the TVA Group and started at Cirque in January of 2001. *What a fun, easy job this will be,* I remember thinking. Having worked at the television network, I thought I knew a lot about the entertainment business. When I told Guy that it shouldn't take me long to get up to speed, he laughed. "Cirque is like no other company you can even imagine," he said. "So take your time. It will take you at least a year to understand how things work around here."

As it turns out, Guy was giving me too much credit. It would actually take several years before I fully understood the many facets of this crazy business.

First, there is the intricate and unique process of developing new shows that live up to Cirque's impossibly high standards, which I will discuss later in this chapter and beyond. Then there is the challenge of keeping our existing shows fresh and exciting while managing the crises that inevitably crop up when producing dozens of live shows daily. Plus, there is the sheer complexity of arranging show tours on five continents around the world: choosing the right cities; finding sites that can accommodate our big-top tents; dealing with local authorities to obtain necessary permits; handling immigration papers for more than a hundred cast and crew; transporting literally tons of gear by airplanes and trucks and making sure all the technology works. No other live-entertainment company tours the globe with such a massive infrastructure, and nobody pushes the envelope of creativity as far as we do. That's why no amount of experience could have possibly prepared me for my new job. At some meetings, I would look around the room and realize that I literally had no idea what everybody was talking about.

That's not even counting the turmoil I found inside the company, caused by the recent departure of two of the most important players in Cirque's history thus far: director Franco Dragone and cofounder Daniel Gauthier.

By the time I arrived, Cirque had grown to seven shows: three resident productions (*Mystère* and *O* in Las Vegas and *La Nouba* at Walt Disney World in Orlando) and four touring shows: *Saltimbanco*, *Alegria*, *Quidam*, and *Dralion*. Though Guy Laliberté has always been the most important force behind Cirque and helped guide every production, as CEO he was busy overseeing the entire operation and had not personally directed shows since the company's earliest days. That job fell to Dragone, the Italian theater director who created every single Cirque show during an impressive run of twelve years, starting with the touring production *La Magie Continue* in 1986 and ending with *O* and *La Nouba* in 1998.

Dragone had an almost mythical reputation within Cirque as the creative genius who could do no wrong. When he left to start his own production company—first creating a hit Celine Dion show and then *Le Rêve*, a water show, at the Wynn Las Vegas—there was tremendous anxiety about the company's future. Even the success of the first show after Dragone's departure—1999's *Dralion*, directed by Guy Caron—could not calm rampant fears that Cirque's best days were over.

Daniel Gauthier's departure triggered a different kind of worry. Having known Guy since high school, he became involved with Cirque early, then handled the business end of things as company president since 1990. He also owned half the company. Within Cirque, Gauthier was considered the sober realist who kept Guy's artistic impulses in check when the numbers didn't add up. That was hardly the whole story, since Guy is also tremendously smart about business. But those perceptions were so strong that employees feared that Guy—having bought out Gauthier's shares and now owning 100 percent of the company—would take too many risks and overspend Cirque into bankruptcy.

With those two crucial figures gone, nobody knew if the company could survive. That was the pressure cooker I had walked into. Years later, I can see that it was probably best that I didn't fully appreciate how much turbulence and anxiety Cirque was experiencing. Had I known, I'm not sure I would have taken the job! And that led to a surprising realization: when you have a big decision to make, sometimes ignorance is bliss.

To be clear, I would never argue against doing due diligence before accepting a job or entering into a business partnership. But there are moments when it's wise to take whatever information you can gather with a grain of salt. Creative endeavors always contain risk. Knowing too much can be as counterproductive as knowing too little, especially if the fear of a daunting challenge keeps you from pursuing your dreams.

STAND UP FOR YOUR BELIEFS

My job was not to replace Daniel Gauthier—not yet anyway. His title had been higher than mine, and I had yet to prove myself within the organization. But I was expected to provide some of the executive experience the company lost when he departed. Most importantly, Guy had a specific project for me: to fulfill his grand vision of an ambitious real-estate venture we called the Cirque du Soleil Complex.

Given his humble beginnings in a small street troupe, Guy was as surprised as anyone at how big Cirque had grown. Believing we had saturated the market for live shows, he wanted to diversify into real estate. Over the years, he had grown frustrated watching other companies make plenty of money investing in property. He loved real estate and wanted to partner with developers to build a series of branded entertainment complexes in various cities around the world, each one anchored by a spectacular resident show.

"Right now you go to a Cirque du Soleil show, you are inspired about the experience, then you walk away from the big top and you are back to reality," Guy said in an interview, laying out his vision. But when visiting the Complex Cirque, customers would leave our shows and enter a hotel, restaurant, nightclub, spa, retail store, museum, or art gallery, each specially designed by Cirque—perhaps with staff or characters dressed up in costumes—to keep them immersed in our surreal world.

Eventually, there would be a Complex Cirque in places like Hong Kong, Tokyo, Singapore, Sydney, and New York. The first would be in London. The idea was to redevelop the Battersea Power Station, a massive iconic landmark located on a forty-acre plot on the banks of the Thames. Built in 1933 to demonstrate England's industrial power, it had an Art Deco turbine control room with parquet floors and a majestic hall lined with Italian marble. Though it closed in 1983 and fell into disrepair, the building retained its hold on the public imagination. With its distinctive four white chimneys (making it look like "an upside-down pool table," one newspaper said), it was Europe's largest brick building and was famous for appearing on the cover of Pink Floyd's 1977 album, *Animals*.

For more than a decade, developers had tried, without success, to bring the old structure back to life. In 1993, the Hong Kong investor Victor Hwang bought the property with plans to turn it into a shopping center with an ice-skating rink and movie theater. When that didn't work out, Hwang's real-estate and construction company, Parkview International, began talking to Guy about Complex Cirque. On December 15, 2000, a week after my hiring was announced, Cirque and Parkview announced their exciting plans for the site: a £500 million entertainment complex that would include two hotels and a 2,000-seat auditorium. To whet the public's appetite, Cirque scheduled a staging of its popular touring show *Quidam* in a big-top tent next to the old power station. Construction was to begin within six months.

The whole effort would be spearheaded by a new division of Cirque that I was heading called New Ventures. I was not at all convinced of the premise behind Guy's strategy—there still seemed plenty of demand for new shows—but if he wanted me to work on this deal, that's what I would do. I had only a vague idea of what the Battersea project was all about when I accepted the job. Guy was pressing me for an answer, and I was so excited about the prospect of working for this fun, growing international company that I made the leap without having a chance to investigate the project deeply.

My first hint that something was awry came before I even started at Cirque. Soon after my hiring was announced, Guy called to invite me to London, where he was meeting with Parkview executives and attending the gala premiere of *Quidam*—very important events, since the Battersea project would be my baby. When I politely declined, saying I still had lots of work to finish up at TVA, he suggested that I could fly to London on Friday, attend the meetings and premiere on Saturday, fly back Sunday, and be back at work on Monday. That sounded ridiculous to me—all that flying around for a single day of meetings?—but Guy insisted. Finally, I relented and eventually realized this kind of spur-of-the-moment globe-hopping was quite normal at Cirque (and today pretty much describes my day-to-day existence!).

So I flew with Josette to London, not yet aware that Complex Cirque was one of the main reasons Gauthier had left the company. He was dead set against it, and I began to see why. At the meeting in Guy's hotel suite, all kinds of wild ideas for the complex were being tossed around. Maybe it could have an interactive museum devoted to Formula One racing, one of Guy's great passions. Or maybe a new attraction in partnership with the Beatles, since Guy had recently become friendly with George Harrison. While everybody was talking excitedly about all the creative possibilities, I kept interrupting to ask some basic questions, trying to understand the business model. Mostly, I was met with blank stares or a quick change of subject.

After the meeting, we all went to the premiere of *Quidam*, a glitzy affair with celebrity guests. That's when I noticed an enormous line of taxicabs and realized Battersea had no parking or public transportation. *How on earth are people supposed to affordably get to Complex Cirque?* I wondered. The whole project seemed thrown together with minimal thought and planning, and the whole day had such a loose, improvised feel that Josette finally said, "What kind of zoo are you joining?"

Back in Montreal after the New Year, I started my job at Cirque and over the next few months began looking closely at the details of this venture. What I found gave me a sick feeling in the pit of my stomach. At just that moment, a financial analyst working on the project, Annie Derome, rushed into my office and said, "Daniel, do you understand this Battersea project won't work?" Relieved that I wasn't the only one worried, I asked her to sit down and explain.

In a nutshell, the developers needed us a lot more than we needed them. Cirque's brand name would make the site a hot destination and satisfy government authorities who required cultural attractions before they would grant the necessary incentives and permits. As far as Parkview was concerned, our shows could be a loss leader because their main function was to lure customers to the hotels, shops, and restaurants. So while the developers stood to profit substantially as owners of the property, Cirque as the anchor tenant would assume tremendous risk: there was no evidence that such a remote site with lousy transportation could support a resident show as more established entertainment centers such as Las Vegas and Orlando do. And if we didn't make money on ticket sales and merchandise, we wouldn't make any money at all.

Now I knew why Gauthier had put his foot down and told Guy, "If you go ahead with this crazy project, you will destroy Cirque du Soleil!"

When I told Guy the same thing, he looked at me with curiosity and said, "You know you are running yourself out of a job, don't you?"

"Yes, I know, but I will find another job," I said. "I just don't want to be known as the guy who put Cirque du Soleil into bankruptcy."

Guy paused for a moment, then said, "Tell you what: Let's go to London and meet with the developers. If you're right, we'll walk away. If I'm right, we'll do the deal."

I agreed, and we flew to London. At the meeting, Guy took control, asking the Parkview executives if Cirque would participate in any of the real-estate profits. The answer was no.

"Strike one," Guy whispered to me.

The next question was about intellectual property. Again, wrong answer.

"Strike two," Guy said.

The last question was about financing. Wrong again.

Guy jumped out of his chair and said, "Strike three, we're out."

Guy was disappointed, but he was extremely grateful that we had avoided a disaster. And I was learning something important—not only about my boss, but about the creative process in general. When Guy proposed something, I realized, the correct answer was never "No." It was "Yes, I will explore it." And that's the right approach with any new idea, no matter who comes up with it. The manager of any creative enterprise should push everyone to explore every avenue possible to turn a new idea—even a crazy one—into reality. If you investigate all possibilities and the project *still* does not make sense, it deserves to die. That's what happened with the Battersea development. Guy pushed it hard, but once he understood that it was based on smoke and mirrors, he turned on a dime and said, "Okay, let's move on."

But that created another problem for me. The big project Guy had hired me to lead had just gone up in smoke. For months, I had worked on Battersea exclusively and knew nothing about how the rest of the business operated. Therefore, I had no job.

When the meeting was over, we left the building and Guy lit up a cigarette. "So now let's talk about what you are going to do next for Cirque "

"Hold on," I said. "Don't feel obligated to offer me a new job. As I told you before, I'm ready to leave. Battersea didn't work out, so there's really nothing for me to—"

"No, you are not leaving," Guy said firmly. "I like the way you approach things, your ideas for growing the company. I know it's a difficult environment right now, with lots of people jockeying for position, but I want to promote you to chief operating officer of the whole company."

I was stunned. In a moment, I went from the unemployment line to one of the top positions at the company, overseeing everything except the development of new shows. Guy wanted the excellent Lyn Heward to continue to report directly to him as head of the Creative Content Division—and that was fine with me. I knew very little about show development and was glad it was in such capable hands. But I was eager to learn about it as well as every other facet of the company.

This was a huge lesson for me: when the stakes are high, stand up for what you believe—even when it seems to contradict what the boss wants. Creative companies generate lots of great ideas, but not all of them make financial sense. One exercise I use is to start with the assumption that I am wrong. It's much too easy to say "I'm right" and then list all the reasons why. It's harder to make the case against my position, then see if I can disprove it. That makes it easier for me to convince people on the other side because now I thoroughly understand their position.

You must pick your battles, of course. There's no need to put your job on the line over a trivial matter. And your research must be rock-solid (your argument based on fact, not opinion). But if the project is important, and your position is well documented, you are not doing your bosses any favors by telling them what you think they want to hear. Plus, you certainly don't want to be known as the villain who damaged the company by pushing a flawed project.

What I am advocating certainly carries some risk—your job may hang in the balance—but the alternative can be worse. Before my arrival, some at Cirque had been trying to convince Guy not only that the Battersea project could work, but that revenues from a chain of Cirque du Soleil Complexes all over the world would eventually dwarf those of our live shows. They had pumped Guy up so much about the potential that it was hard for me to bring him back down to the core business.

Fortunately, Guy was open minded enough to hear me out. Meanwhile, those other people provided a cautionary tale about telling the boss what they think he wants to hear: today, they are no longer with the company.

DON'T BE A SALESPERSON

Guy did not give up the Complex Cirque idea right away—over the years, we continued exploring the concept in London, Montreal, Las Vegas, and other cities—but the projects never came to fruition for the same reason each time: Cirque du Soleil is not a real-estate developer. We are an entertainment company that is most successful when we stick to what we do well: creating and producing astonishing shows.

Beyond *Mystère* and *O*, I had no idea how many more of our shows could thrive in Las Vegas. But I felt certain that if our productions were distinctive and dazzling enough, the crowds would come. As for our big-top tours, we had not yet explored hundreds of cities around the world, enormous markets just waiting to be tapped.

Guy supported my plan to expand our core business, but it was a challenge to convince others inside the company that sustained growth would not happen with risky diversification projects. Even after several months, I was the unproven newcomer with few allies. Preoccupied with Battersea, I had not yet integrated myself into the company and still knew almost nothing about how the business operated. On most days, I felt like an outsider, a feeling heightened by certain executives who wanted my job and made subtle and not-so-subtle efforts to undermine me.

During most of my first year, in fact, I seemed like a bad fit for the artistic culture of Cirque. With my background, I was accustomed to acting like a salesman. Give me a proposal and a roomful of businesspeople, and I could win them over. Problem was, at Cirque, they hate salespeople! Whenever I went into my pitch—at big meetings, small gatherings, or chance encounters—I would get scowls of annoyance and plenty of pushback. Nobody paid the least bit of attention to what I was saying because they so distrusted my slick approach. To them, I sounded phony and manipulative.

Finally, I realized what was happening and gained another valuable lesson: to thrive in a creative environment, drop the sales talk. I had to learn how to listen more, be less aggressive, and speak more openly, from the heart. Once I did that, it was much easier to fit in, gain supporters, and move my initiatives forward. Best of all, I found myself looking forward to coming to work and began enjoying my job for the first time.

LEARN THE BUSINESS

It wasn't until the Battersea project ended that I began to understand the creative heartbeat that drove the company. And yet I needed to know so much more. I became hungry for information, wanting to know everything about how the whole apparatus operates, on every level—pull back the curtain, you might say, to understand how Cirque du Soleil creates the miracles we see onstage.

The advice I am offering here—"Learn the Business"— might seem obvious, but you'd be surprised at how often even top executives do not have a complete understanding of what goes on inside their companies. They might have a general idea, but I'm talking about something else: a highly detailed, granular knowledge of every aspect of the organization. This is especially crucial in creative companies because it shows you possess traits valued by the culture—qualities like empathy, curiosity, intelligence, and compassion. Everyone in the company can benefit from learning about the rest of the business, from entry-level staff hoping for advancement to upper management who are showing they genuinely care about their employees and what they do.

Over the next few months, I learned about everything from casting to costumes to the audition process. I watched rehearsals for hours, taking notes. During breaks, I would ask the cast and crew, "What does this piece of technology do? How do these acrobats train? Why does *this* act work but *that* one doesn't?" Even subtle things became important, like how to behave when seeing artists backstage or in the kitchen tent as they gather for meals. Today, after a show, I'll say, "You guys have taken pictures with me a zillion times—but let's do it again, and make sure everybody's in it." We laugh about it, but the point is that this learning process is about more than just gaining information. It brings you deep into the culture and creates strong relationships.

When a new employee starts at Cirque, one of my first bits of advice is, "Never ever call a touring show on a Monday." That's when our shows are dark, the only day of the week the cast and crew have off. If you bother them on a Monday, they'll laugh at your cluelessness and freeze you out. Investigating your company deeply can dig up details like that, which can spell the difference between being embraced by your coworkers or not.

BRING IN OUTSIDE TALENT

It was the fall of 2001, after being at Cirque for nine or ten months, that I began this learning process. It was an especially fascinating—and anxious—time because the company was still in the throes of the existential crisis triggered by Franco Dragone's departure. After doing things a certain way for fifteen years—Dragone directing, with Guy's oversight—we suddenly had to develop a new way to produce shows.

This turned out to be an opportunity in disguise when Guy came up with a brilliant solution: bring in a new director from the outside for each new show. It takes nothing away from Dragone's accomplishments to say that the string of hits that followed his departure, in what some refer to as Cirque's golden years— *Varekai, Zumanity, KÀ, Corteo, The Beatles LOVE, Michael Jackson ONE*, and more—showed how stimulating it can be for a company to bring in outside talent with fresh perspectives on what your product can be.

Until then, our focus on launching new shows carried the risk that each production would seem too similar to the last one. Bringing in outside directors solved that problem. Each new show bore the signature of a particular director, thus diversifying our content.

As we experimented with this new process, however, we knew it carried its own set of risks. The newcomer would know nothing about how the company operates, and teaching them would be tremendously costly and time consuming. In our case, many of the directors we considered were top talent from the worlds of theater, opera, dance, and music but had zero experience with circus acts.

Another issue: Once you invite these outsiders in, how do you keep them on track and make sure they get the job done? We can encourage wild creativity and fresh ways of approaching a show, but that does not mean anything goes. We still needed a process to create high-quality productions, recognizably Cirque, within our defined budget and time frame. There had to be a delicate balancing act, in other words, between the outrageously creative and the rigorously practical.

Our solution was to team the outside directors with two long-time staff members—a director of creation and a director of production—to help them translate their artistic vision into reality. They would serve as guides who set up the parameters of the sandbox and then let the director play.

The director of creation is responsible for offering up all the personnel the director might need, from casting and costumes to performers and coaches. "Do you want a skateboarder here?" they might say. "Or a trapeze artist? Or maybe we should create an entirely new apparatus for the acrobats to perform on?"

Meanwhile, the director of production makes sure the show stays within budget and on schedule. This person is an expert on getting things done and knows how to manage a typical $30 million Cirque budget. For example, with touring shows, the equipment must fit inside the fifty trucks we have available, no more. "If you want ten musicians, fine," the director of production might say, "but you'll have to cut two acrobats." This creates efficiencies, cutting off ideas that we can't afford or that won't work in the given time frame.

As you can imagine, inventing a new show is an elaborate process, taking about two years for a touring production. Resident shows take longer, usually three years, because we must also oversee the construction of the theater, which can be an enormous job. Just consider the massive water-tank stage for *O* at the Bellagio or the giant rotating stage for *KÀ* at the MGM Grand.

Cirque's first production under our new system was the touring show *Varekai*. By the time I got involved, the show was already deep in rehearsals and only six months away from its premiere in Montreal in the spring of 2002. Guy chose as director Dominic Champagne, an award-winning Canadian playwright and theater director who had designed and directed many prestigious public events, including several editions of Quebec's national holiday celebrations. Dominic had never created a circus show before, but that wasn't a problem—we would provide that expertise. Guy was looking for someone with a fresh artistic vision who was excited about the chance to use circus arts to execute it.

This process of recruiting outside talent and teaming them with guides from within the company is something any business can do. If I were chief executive of a car company, for example, I would hire accomplished engineers and designers who had never made cars before to see what they came up with. They would not have to know anything about building engines because we would already have experts to do that. Instead, I'd want that designer to focus exclusively on making the most creative, functional, fashionable car possible.

If that approach sounds fanciful, consider that business history is full of hit products that emerge from entirely different fields: bubble wrap was originally a new kind of textured wallpaper until someone thought to use it for protecting items during shipping. The Slinky was a stabilizing device for ships before someone knocked it over, watched it walk across a desk, and discovered a new toy. Viagra was invented to lower blood pressure and treat heart disease until researchers realized it had another powerful effect. You will never know what brilliant products are out there, undiscovered, until you open your company's doors and minds to new possibilities.

GIVE CREATORS A MANDATE

In business, as in life, you can't just tell people, "Go be creative. Come back to me with a fantastic new idea." That leads to wasting time and resources and results in ideas your company doesn't want or can't use.

Instead, give your creative team a mandate—some direction about the kind of ideas you are looking for. In the case of *Varekai*, the mandate was broad but helped Dominic think about what the show could be: Guy wanted a different kind of story, unlike what Cirque had done so far. He also did not want to repeat the same acrobatic acts as previous shows, so he told his creative team to recruit new talent to offer something different.

After giving it some thought, Dominic came back with an idea: The acrobatic acts in Cirque are often about flight, but how about a story about falling? When Dominic was young, he fell from a tree and broke his leg, unable to walk for many months. The experience was quite traumatic. How about reimagining the myth of Icarus by starting the show with the brash young man's fall back to Earth?

ALLOW CREATIVE FREEDOM

The director of creation, Andrew Watson, and the director of production, Stephane Mongeau, loved the idea, and Guy approved it as well. They liked the fact that Dominic's story had personal meaning for him, though they also knew that everything would depend on the execution.

Given Guy's artistic genius, charisma, and strong opinions, I was surprised at how much creative freedom he allowed his team. It's not uncommon for leaders to impose their vision on a project from the beginning, but at Cirque the process is quite the opposite. After hiring Dominic, Guy stepped aside to give him free rein to develop his idea.

That was a big takeaway for me, confirming what I knew from my own experience at TVA: It's so important for the talent to know they can create and dream without interference from above. Management must understand that it exists to serve the creators, not the other way around.

That said, there are parameters the creative team must work within when developing a new show. For touring productions, there are usually two acts of fifty minutes each, separated by an intermission. Each half contains five or six acts, which we call the show's "acrobatic skeleton" (something of a misnomer because the acts are not all acrobatics—some feature dancers, jugglers, or clowns).

In devising the acts, the director assembles a creative team of specialists that includes set designers, costume designers, composers, choreographers, lighting designers, sound designers, and more—about twenty people who immediately get to work brainstorming ideas and then meet regularly to discuss their progress. Performers are hired through an elaborate casting process to find the best artists and athletes in the world, which I will discuss in a later chapter. Upon arriving at our facility in Montreal, they undergo months of training to learn their routines, develop their characters, and learn specific skills, like how to apply their own makeup.

As the show is being assembled, everyone from directors to cast members are given a great deal of freedom to express themselves artistically. That's the best way to keep employees in any company inspired and engaged—by making them feel that they are not just following orders but using their creativity to put a personal stamp on their job. That's a big reason why audiences are so mesmerized by our shows. When dozens of incredibly talented and dedicated artists come together under one tent to fully express themselves, the result is magic.

MONITOR THE CREATIVE PROCESS

In a business context, providing creative freedom does not mean having no clue about what the product is until it's finished and ready to offer to customers. That's a recipe for disaster. The solution is to periodically monitor the process to make sure the product is marketable, consistent with your brand, and sufficiently original to maintain your company's reputation as an innovative leader.

As I watched *Varekai* develop, I was intrigued by Cirque's use of "checkpoints" at various stages of a show's development. That's when Guy watches each act and reviews the entire acrobatic skeleton to see what is working and what needs fixing. At the beginning, checkpoints happen once a month. In the three months leading up to the premiere, they come every two weeks. A few weeks before opening night, when rehearsals have moved to the big-top tent, checkpoints occur every two days, then nightly during the final week.

When assessing a show's progress, pacing is very important. The show should open strong to get the audience involved—making them sit up and cry "Wow!" That's followed by something less intense because it's exhausting for the audience to be subjected to a nonstop adrenaline rush. It might be a clown act for a bit of comic relief that allows the crew time to prepare for the next act. Clowning is actually the most difficult part of any show because so much of it depends on audience interaction, something not possible until near the end of the process, when rehearsals move into the big-top tent. The end of the first half and the very end of each show should close with a big "Wow!"

During rehearsals of *Varekai*, it was clear that a great deal was riding on this show. Trying to prove that Cirque could step out from under the shadow of Franco Dragone put tremendous pressure on Dominic, his creative leadership team, and the whole cast and crew. They knew Guy would not accept anything half-baked.

At one checkpoint, Guy got his first look at a new apparatus Dominic's team had created called the "multiple trapeze." It was a tall rectangular structure that looked like an enormous jungle gym and featured six artists climbing and hanging on the bars as music played.

"I don't like the act at all," Guy said when it was over, the creative team gathered around him in the studio. "We never see their full bodies. The structure looks like a pile of scrap metal. It's not just one or two people inside the structure—there are six of them! I won't have six people in an act unless it makes me say, 'Wow!'"

But rather than kill the act on the spot, he gave the team another chance. I found this strategy intriguing. Many times, after a rehearsal, I would tell Guy, "This act just doesn't work!" He would say, "I know, but give them a chance. If it still doesn't work in a week or two, we will kill it. But first I want to give them the opportunity to show me that they are right and I am wrong." If the team managed to bring the act to life, Guy was open minded enough to keep it. He could also tell when a new act was not fatally flawed but simply needed more time to develop.

In the case of the multiple trapeze, the team tried again at the next checkpoint. It still didn't work and was scrapped. The performers were crushed, having poured their heart and soul into that routine for three months. But some could see Guy's point. "Actually, I can understand that," said Raquel Karro Oliveira, a Brazilian aerialist. "I almost agree with him if I think about myself as an audience member."

The multiple trapeze was a valiant attempt to fulfill Guy's mandate to bring in new acrobatic acts. Dominic and his team had better luck with a new "strap act," a form of aerial acrobatics in which performers wrap a strap around their hands and wrists and soar through the air performing twists, rolls, and various other stunning maneuvers. This is normally a solo act, but the new wrinkle was the use of a pair of British identical twin gymnasts, Kevin and Andrew Atherton.

Bringing in the Atherton twins was a big adjustment for everybody. Though the brothers had often competed against each other in gymnastics events, they had never worked together in a circus act before. Now they would have to catch each other as they flew high above the stage and audience without a safety net.

Cirque, meanwhile, had never created a two-person strap act before. Dominic and his team started off by asking the twins to demonstrate their aerial skills. Then they told them which ones they liked best and left the brothers alone to create a routine. As they watched the results, the coaches and directors suggested changes and tweaks. In the months that followed, they all worked tirelessly to revise and refine the act until they eventually came up with a seven-minute act that was absolutely spectacular.

The monitoring process had done its job—weeding out the weak acts from the strong ones and keeping the development process on track, on schedule, and under budget. There were still whispers of doubt in the halls of Cirque as people said *Varekai* would never reach the level of a Franco Dragone show. But I felt good about what I was seeing. As the months went by, the rehearsals seemed to inch closer to fulfilling Guy's mandate: creating a show that was identifiably Cirque du Soleil but entirely original, surprising, and astonishing in its own way.

WEAR THE SHOES OF THE CUSTOMER

As I watched the Atherton twins rehearse their routine—soaring high above me, flying apart then coming together—I no longer felt like an executive at Cirque du Soleil doing my job. Suddenly, I was a member of the audience, speechless and awestruck by what I was witnessing.

That's a lesson for every leader: put yourself in the shoes of your customers, of course, but don't stop there; make it impossible to look at your product any other way. In the rehearsal studio, it took no effort for me to transform into a spectator. In fact, I could not have resisted the spell of the magnificent Atherton twins even if I tried.

I realized that, in the end, it doesn't matter what I think of a show anyway. All that matters is what the audience thinks. That's why during intermission of a touring show, I like to disappear into the crowd, eavesdropping on their conversations. That's the best market research I've ever encountered: just listening to comments about what people loved or didn't love about the show, yet another way to step into the shoes of the customer.

BE AGILE

During one checkpoint, Guy thought the second act was too slow and needed something dazzling. So Dominic went to the casting department, looked at the bios and videos of several candidates, and said, "Please call them to see who's available."

That seemed like a normal part of the creative process. But it was mid-April of 2002, three days before our Montreal premiere!

I couldn't believe it. Seventy-two hours before opening night?! I literally started sweating. I was not used to this, not at all. In a traditional business, you carefully develop a plan and then stick with it. You don't radically revamp your product three days before bringing it to market!

Putting on a live show, I was learning, is not like manufacturing widgets. There are so many human variables that can change from one rehearsal to the next that it's impossible to know how all the acts will flow together, and what emotional response they will elicit from the audience, until the production is very far along. This is especially true for our touring productions that don't actually rehearse in the big-top tent until three to six months before opening night, depending on the complexity of the acts.

On the other hand, tinkering too much carries its own risks. Even minor changes can alter the flow of the show and the delicate balance between acts. Any surgery must be done with extreme care.

Within hours, Dominic chose a Mexican juggler named Octavio Alegria, but it would take him two days to travel to Montreal. That left us just one day of rehearsal. We had watched videos of his juggling act, he came well recommended, and he was considered "ready to go" in Cirque vernacular. Still, I was stunned—the premiere was tomorrow!

As the final rehearsal approached, I was a bundle of nerves. That soon turned to grateful disbelief as the session went smoothly and professionally. On opening night, Octavio went into his act—a miraculous stunt in which he kept tossing bowling pins, soccer balls, Mexican sombreros, and ping-pong balls in the air and catching them with his hands, feet, and head. In one astonishing sequence, he juggled four or five ping-pong balls in his mouth, spitting them up and catching them, one after another. Once again, I became a stunned spectator: "How on earth . . . ?!!" In the thrilling finale, he tossed the sombreros high in the air and caught each one, diving across the floor to snag the last hat just before it hit the floor.

Our hero got a standing ovation that night. And every night after that.

After surviving such a heart-stopping episode, it would be natural for a new executive like me to call an emergency meeting and propose a complete overhaul of the way things are done. I could have drawn up elaborate procedures to identify problems earlier and pledge to never allow this to happen again. But after being here for more than a year, I knew better. My job was to adapt to Cirque's unusual culture, not the other way around. Who was I to tell Cirque du Soleil how to put on a show?

Trying to impose a conventional management style on Cirque, I realized, would be a disaster. *Bureaucracy* is a dirty word around here. Everyone's mentality is "The show must go on!" and we constantly operate with a laser-like focus on making that happen. Nobody sits around writing memos and thinking up new policies and protocols that would only slow everybody down. I realized that many companies with entrenched bureaucracies— including some I used to work for—would benefit from being able to react as calmly and quickly to a crisis as Cirque does.

When the premiere was over, Guy was ecstatic: we had another new hit show. Over the years, *Varekai* would be seen by six million people worldwide. More importantly, we had proven that Cirque could thrive using a variety of directorial voices. "Daniel, we will never ever be held hostage by one director anymore!" Guy said. "Now we will be truly independent and control our own future."

That future would be based not on distracting diversification projects but groundbreaking new shows and expanding to new markets around the world. Neither of us knew it, but we were at the dawn of a new age at Cirque.

BEWARE OF CONTROVERSIAL TOPICS

No sooner had *Varekai* opened than my attention was consumed by our next project, a resident production already under development. We had less than eighteen months to finish creating the show and oversee the construction of the theater at the New York–New York Hotel & Casino in Las Vegas before opening in September of 2003.

Guy's mandate for this show could be summed up in a single word: *sexy*. Las Vegas has a long history of sexual attractions, of course, from prostitution to strip joints, but at the time there were no classy, artistic, cabaret-style shows. Guy felt it was time. For the past decade, Vegas had evolved from its seedy roots into a sophisticated dining, shopping, and entertainment destination. When Cirque opened its first show there—*Mystère* in 1993—gambling accounted for 85 percent of business revenue. Over the next nearly three decades, that number dropped to 35 percent. Cirque had a lot to do with that. By 2020, we were the biggest live-entertainment company in the city by far, accounting for about half of ticket sales for all large theatrical shows.

The subject matter of our new show, called *Zumanity*, was a tremendous risk for Cirque, given that all our previous shows had been family-friendly (the title was a neologism derived from *zoo* and *humanity*). But Guy could not resist the creative challenge and the chance to demonstrate that each new Cirque show would not simply be a carbon copy of the last one. And we signed up someone we thought would be the perfect director: Philippe Decouflé, a French choreographer, dancer, mime, and theater director who had created the 1992 Winter Olympics ceremonies in Albertville, France, and sexy cabaret shows in Paris. *Zumanity*, billed as "another side of Cirque du Soleil," would feature erotic songs, dance, acrobatics, and comedy strictly for adults only.

I soon learned how difficult it can be to create a show with such a controversial theme. There are certain subjects in life— politics, religion, race—that trigger such powerful reactions that finding common ground can be nearly impossible. That's true whether we're talking about twelve hundred people in a Las Vegas theater or members of the creative team itself.

Our checkpoint process exposed this problem well before the show opened: Philippe and his team were producing a much darker and more chaotic show than what Guy had in mind. Sometimes directors can make adjustments to fix problems like that. At other times, they are simply too deeply invested in their vision to make the necessary changes. In this case, it was the latter. This was nobody's fault; Philippe simply wasn't the right director for this particular project. He was far better suited for two other, highly successful Cirque shows he directed later: the resident shows *Iris* in Los Angeles in 2011 and *Paramour* in New York in 2016, which moved to Hamburg, Germany, three years later.

In August of 2002, we announced a new director: the Quebec actor, playwright, and theater director René Richard Cyr.

But René also struggled, unable to find the right tone for such a volatile subject. I had been at Cirque for more than two years by that time and had never seen the company so lost. By the summer of 2003, only a few months before the premiere, our partner, MGM Resorts International, was getting nervous, expecting us to deliver a hit show for its theater that we were not even close to achieving. "Maybe we just got lucky with *Varekai*," some inside the company whispered. "Maybe bringing in outside directors was not such a great idea after all."

KNOW YOUR BRAND

Desperate to save the production, we approached Dominic Champagne. Not only had he mastered Cirque's creative process while making *Varekai*, but he and René were good friends. Perhaps they could fix the show together. After much back-and-forth, they agreed.

Dominic tried to insert more humor into *Zumanity*, and the show improved. But there simply wasn't enough time to do the complete overhaul it needed. As a result, nobody was happy with the show when it opened on September 20—including some audience members, who stormed out after only a few minutes.

For me, the lesson was clear: know your brand. Your customers certainly do. For nearly twenty years, the Cirque du Soleil logo meant spectacular, inspiring, family-oriented entertainment, like *Mystère* or *O*. That's not what people got, and many left the New York–New York theater feeling insulted and cheated. We failed to do what industry leaders do well—find a common denominator to reach a broad cross section of the market.

One problem was our advertising. Calling it "another side of Cirque du Soleil" was too subtle. We revamped our campaign to make clear this was X-rated adult entertainment. But by then, much of the damage had been done. Because the misunderstanding was our fault, we went out of our way to apologize and reimburse customers or invite them to another show. We didn't try to be right and blame the audience for not "getting it." That's a trap companies can easily fall into—getting defensive, avoiding responsibility, and forgetting that the customer is always right. If people felt we misrepresented *Zumanity*, we did not argue. We simply took care of them.

A bigger problem was the show itself. We were learning the profound difference between *sex* and *sexy*. *Zumanity* was too much about sexual acts themselves, too dirty and dark. We needed to stop taking ourselves so seriously and be more playful. In a word, the show needed to be *sexier*. Few people sitting in a theater will agree on what sex is or should be. It's much easier to reach a consensus on what sexy is, especially when it's portrayed as a party. We needed to approach this universal activity as a fun game that anybody can play; that was the common denominator.

It took nearly a year after the show opened, but Dominic and his team finally made that transition. *Zumanity* became a funny, X-rated show with stunning acrobatics that remains entirely consistent with our brand. A group of women, or guys, could show up, have some drinks, and know they'd have a great time. For nearly two decades, the show was sold out almost every night until 2020, when it became a casualty of the pandemic.

EARN THE RIGHT TO ASSERT YOURSELF

Zumanity marked another turning point in my own evolution within the company. If *Varekai* was my chance to learn the business, *Zumanity* was when I began to assert myself. Finally, I felt comfortable regularly expressing my point of view—not in front of the creative team, but to Guy directly. (He wanted to be the one delivering the critique so that the creative team would not be confused by mixed signals.)

When animal-rights activists began complaining about our use of a snake in *Zumanity*, I saw my opening. Cirque has long been famous for not using animals in its shows, but, given the irresistible Adam and Eve connotations, we decided to make an exception. The loud objections from activists began after opening night and did not let up.

When I told Guy that we didn't need all this negative publicity just as the show was opening, he said, "Don't worry; it will pass." Based on my experience in public relations, I felt he was wrong. "The drumbeat will only get louder," I told him. "We have an issue here, and it's so easy to fix. Just get rid of the goddamn snake!"

Guy burst out laughing. "Okay, I guess we will have barbecued snake tonight!" Out went the controversial reptile, the animal-rights folks were happy, and I had notched my first major victory. (Don't worry; he was kidding about the barbecue.)

Spending so much time soaking up the culture and operations of Cirque gave me a great deal of credibility when it came time to make my voice heard. People knew I was not some know-it-all who jumped in on day one telling everybody what to do. Yes, it's good to be assertive in professional situations, but it's more important to know what you're talking about before you do.

PUSH THE BOUNDARIES OF CREATIVITY

Cirque's deal with MGM was that we agreed to its request for an average-sized show (*Zumanity*) if we could also do a much larger, expensive production at another of its Las Vegas properties. So, as we were putting *Zumanity* together, we were simultaneously hard at work on an exciting new project. MGM wanted a big, flashy resident production for its flagship resort, the MGM Grand. With nearly seven thousand rooms, it was the largest hotel complex in the world when it opened in 1993. Our mandate was to create something as iconic and enduring for the MGM Grand as *O* has been for the Bellagio.

Our strategy of growing the company by launching more new shows created a challenge: each new production had to be radically different than the others. Otherwise, why bother? Especially in Las Vegas, a new show that was too similar would simply eat into the sales of our existing shows. So we had to push the limits of creativity further than we ever had before. That meant hiring directors with a singular vision, artists who would lead us into exciting, perhaps even dangerous, new territory.

As we discussed the new show for the MGM Grand, one word kept coming up: *epic*. Guy had always been fascinated by martial arts and wanted a big, dramatic story with lots of fight scenes. Most Cirque shows are heavy on spectacle and light on story. This time, we wanted a dramatic story line to draw the audience in; then we'd wow them with the acrobatics.

The best director to execute that mandate, Guy decided, was Robert LePage, the distinguished Quebec playwright, actor, and director of stage and film who had already created acclaimed operas with the epic feel we wanted. At our first meeting with Robert, we were ready for something big and utterly unique. We were not at all prepared for what he was about to suggest.

"Here's the idea," he said. "There will be no stage."

First silence, then nervous laughter. "Come again?" someone said.

"No stage!" Robert said. "Just a big void and then a giant mobile platform rises up from the blackness. It will flip-flop, rotate horizontally and vertically, at some points literally disappear and then pop back up again. Most of the action will take place on several of these platforms—acrobats and martial artists climbing up and down, fighting and falling into the abyss below, that kind of thing."

"Um," someone said. "Does this technology exist?"

"No, there's no such thing," Robert said. "Isn't that great? We'll have to invent it!"

At any previous moment of my professional life, I would have suggested that the man seek counseling. But I took it as a sign of my progress in adapting to Cirque's culture that I instantly became intrigued and began thinking about how we might fulfill his vision.

I was not surprised that Guy did not bat an eye. "Great," he said, "let's see if we can make it work!"

It's hard to overstate what a huge undertaking it was to create the show that became known as *KÀ* (an ancient Egyptian word for the human spirit that survives death). Creating Robert's moving stage ended up taking more than three years, costing $200 million, and pushing several teams of brilliant engineers to their exasperated limits. They had to find a way to take mammoth hydraulic lifts—the kinds that ships use to load and unload cargo—and repurpose them for our show. In the end, two giant moving platforms were constructed inside the theater, one looking like the mysterious monolith in *2001: A Space Odyssey*, and there were five smaller lifts that appeared to float through a bottomless space.

As we began choreographing the action that would play out on these moving stages, I felt exhilarated by the process and wondered how many revolutionary ideas were being missed by companies every day because they lacked the imagination or courage to attempt projects that seemed impossible. Even after scoring a big hit, firms often became overly cautious, afraid of squandering their success by taking more risks. Innovators like Steve Jobs prove there is another way. He never felt content with changing the world just once with the Macintosh computer, or again with the iPod, or yet again with the iPad tablet, so he came out with the earthshaking iPhone. Elon Musk is another irrepressible pioneer—not satisfied with merely moving the entire automobile industry toward electric cars with Tesla but also striving to bring people to Mars with his SpaceX rocket-ship company.

What made these leaders different from the very beginning is not just that they dared to dream big. It's that they understood a fundamental truth about modern business: their companies' very future depended on nurturing those dreams and turning them into reality. That's how Cirque looks at its business, starting with a question every company can ask itself: How far can I expand the boundaries of creativity today?

THE SERIOUS POINT OF FUN

None of this is to suggest that shooting for the moon is easy. Building the movable stage for *KÀ* was such an extraordinary challenge—something that no theatrical company had ever attempted—that the inevitable cost overruns and delays began to stack up. Guy and I spent much of our time explaining to our partners at MGM why this production was so expensive and why the opening date kept getting pushed back.

At one point, the chief executive of MGM Grand, John Redmond, became so concerned about *KÀ* that he scheduled a video conference with Guy and me. "When are you going to open the show?" he demanded, not for the first time.

"We will open when it's ready," Guy replied.

"Can you be a little bit more precise?"

"No," Guy said. "We're having a few issues with the technology and want to make sure it's working perfectly before we open it to the public."

"Well, keep me posted because I'm under a lot of pressure here." A whole lineup of high-end restaurants, some by celebrity chefs, had already opened at the resort, John reminded us. Without crowds from our show, they were becoming a sad scene of empty tables.

The call ended without any yelling or dramatics. Our relationship with MGM has always been warm and respectful. But the message was clear: with our partner losing millions every month the theater stayed dark, this crazy stage idea needed to work.

All creative ventures have elements of uncertainty, which can generate tremendous stress in a business context. How to handle that pressure? I found it instructive to watch Guy's response. One night in particular comes to mind. *KÀ* had finally launched in previews, but there were still lots of kinks to work out. The audience streamed into the theater before the show to find a huge, empty pit where the stage should be, smoke rising from the depths and spooky music playing. The goal was to create an ominous but still-exciting feeling before the show started—which it certainly did for me, knowing there was still no guarantee these experimental moving platforms would work reliably.

The cast and crew were tense that night, knowing that Guy and I were in the audience watching. The show began beautifully, but after about half an hour, the platforms stopped moving and the cast dispersed. After an interminable delay, an announcement over the loudspeakers said, "We are sorry, but due to technical difficulties, tonight's show has been canceled. Audience members should please go to the box office for a refund." Seeing my disappointment, Guy shrugged and said, "Get used to it. This happened to us about twenty times when we opened *O*."

Then Guy called the production manager over and said, "Get all the executives and producers and the creative team together. We're all going out to dinner."

When everyone arrived at the restaurant, they were bracing for Guy to yell at them, maybe even fire the whole damn bunch. Instead, he said, "I can tell you all need a drink. You're too nervous, let's loosen up. We're going to have dinner together, and I want you to drink as much wine as you want. Then you will go to bed and sleep late tomorrow because I don't want to see anyone at the theater in the morning. That rehearsal is canceled. Let the technicians work out the problems. Come by in the afternoon, and run this sucker before tomorrow night's show. That's what's important: just run the show and stop worrying about the damn technology."

Everyone looked at each other and smiled, and we had an enjoyable, relaxed dinner together. It was a great lesson in leadership. Behind the fun was a serious point: Guy was letting his team know that he had faith in them, helping them believe that the technology would ultimately work and the show would be fine.

The next day, everyone arrived at the theater refreshed, confident, and optimistic. After lots of tinkering, the moving platforms began to work, and we spent the rest of the preview period getting ready for opening night.

When *KÀ* premiered on November 12, 2004, the reviews were fawning. We were complimented for creating the first Cirque show with a compelling narrative throughout, mind-blowing technical feats, and first-rate acrobatics and martial arts. The *Los Angeles Times* said it "may well be the most lavish production in the history of Western theater. It is surely the most technologically advanced."

After that night, *KÀ* became one of our most profitable productions. Michael Rapino, the CEO of one of our competitors, Live Nation, put it well: "Daniel, I have never seen a show like that, and I'm sure that I will never see a show like that again, ever. Only you guys are crazy enough to create something that big and complicated to operate night after night."

By then, I had been at Cirque for nearly five years. I had learned the business, steeped myself in its culture, found my place, and began to assert myself. Soon, it would be my turn to have a major impact on this company I had grown to love.

CHAPTER 3

TAKE A MAGICAL MYSTERY TOUR

Before I started at Cirque, I would never have considered business networking to be a creative act. Like most executives, I thought a round of golf was the best way to connect with people outside the office, a time to casually get to know them before getting down to business. It never would have occurred to me to do what Guy did: throw an enormous, crazy party.

And I do mean *enormous*. Soon after I came on board, I took a look at our balance sheets and noticed a large expense—$1 million—for the huge bash Guy threw every year at his lakefront mansion near Montreal to celebrate one of his favorite events, the Canadian Grand Prix Formula One car race. I had been to his party the previous year, when I was still at the TVA network. Yes, I remembered the party being fun. But now that I was an executive at Cirque, it seemed like a ridiculous waste of money. "What on earth does that have to do with our mission?" I asked Guy.

"It's my equivalent of your golf course," he replied. Seeing that I wasn't convinced, Guy flashed me his sly grin and said, "Okay, come to the party this year and then you can tell me what you think."

SHOWCASE WHAT YOU DO

It was a Sunday afternoon in June of 2001, just after the con-
clusion of the Formula One race, when I showed up at Guy's
house. His parties had already become legendary in the entertainment world, and being here reminded me why. A thousand
people were streaming through the front door, walking through
his kitchen, and ending up outside in his huge backyard. The
grounds had been meticulously landscaped with custom flower
arrangements, a large pergola, and several Buddha statues. Under
a tree, a nineteen-piece orchestra was playing what sounded like
nineteenth-century European circus music. The sound system
and elaborate lighting were first-rate. The food and drinks were
exquisite, served by a crew of sixty waiters. People of all social
classes were there, from secretaries to race-car drivers. The year
before, Robert De Niro had attended while in Montreal filming
the crime thriller *The Score*.

The entertainment was as spectacular as you would expect
from the founder of Cirque du Soleil: A woman sang opera while
riding a gondola across Guy's private lake. Acrobats executed
incredible stunts, including Chinese artists climbing up long
poles. At one point, Guy appeared on a high platform and performed his old fire-breathing act as the crowd roared.

As I mingled with the other guests, I began to understand
Guy's rationale for the party. The year before, I hardly knew
anyone. This time, I recognized and chatted with dozens of people associated with the company—financiers, event promoters,
talent agents, politicians, entertainers, and business types of all
kinds, a global web of contacts crucial to helping Cirque fulfill
its mission. "Everyone comes to feel good and have an amazing
time," Guy said. "After this, it's much easier to get a deal done."

Now I was starting to get it, and I realized that I had to be open to different ways of doing business. Yes, the party was expensive, but it was actually a more efficient way to accomplish our goals than simply playing golf or meeting at a restaurant for dinner. Guy's celebration was a platform to showcase Cirque's new acts, new sets, new performers, and new technology while bringing our partners close to us in the process.

Most companies would not throw a party like this, of course. But every firm can find original ways to showcase their ingenuity to attract potential buyers or partners. Steve Jobs, for example, was a master of new-product demos as he whipped up the media, industry leaders, and the public into a state of near-ecstasy over his latest devices. Car manufacturers have also become expert at unveiling new models with glitzy shows that create excitement and goodwill. No matter what business you are in, there are great opportunities to find creative ways to showcase what you do and build important relationships.

LET THE NETWORKING BEGIN

What really convinced me about the genius of Guy's annual party, however, was the story he told me about what happened at the previous year's event, when George Harrison showed up.

It seems that Guy knew the ex-Beatle, but only barely, through their shared love of Formula One racing. When they met at races around the world, they would engage in small talk, but never anything more, until a mutual friend invited George to Guy's party after the Montreal race in June of 2000. The legendary musician was not feeling well, having been diagnosed with throat cancer a few years earlier, and his recovery had been set back when he was attacked at his home in London six months earlier by a crazed intruder who repeatedly stabbed him with a knife. Now he was gamely trying to get out more. Their mutual friend Paul Stewart, a former racer and son of legendary Formula One champion Jackie Stewart, finally convinced George to go. "Just have a cocktail and stay for an hour or so," he said.

I didn't see George that night—the party was too crowded, and I had no idea he would be there—but Guy told me later that when George arrived, he was hypnotized by the scene. "I will never forget the look on his face when he entered my magic garden," Guy told me later. "Like he was entering an enchanted forest."

George was especially taken by the music being played by the orchestra under a tree. The group, Fanfare Pourpour, plays original tunes that are hard to categorize, inspired by Federico Fellini, Kurt Weill, jazz, and world music. Guy has known the musicians since he was a teenager in Montreal. When the set was over, George walked up to the band and said, "That's the best music I've heard in years." The musicians, stunned to recognize the famous face, didn't know what to say except, "Merci!"

For the rest of the night, I was told, George remained transfixed by the band. After getting a little tipsy on champagne, he sidled up next to the accordion player, Lou Babin, and gently played some notes on her instrument's keyboard, singing along even though he didn't know the tune. Lou smiled and let him play, enjoying his warmth and playfulness.

At sunrise, before leaving, George told Guy, "That was one of the best times of my life. Thank you for sharing your magical garden with me. I would like to invite you to see my own magical garden. Next time you are in London, please call me. I would love to have you for dinner and spend the afternoon together."

A few months later, Guy was in England on business and went to visit George at Friar Park, his nineteenth-century neo-Gothic mansion in Henley-on-Thames, about an hour west of London. The two spent hours walking around some of the property's sixty-two acres with its caves, grottoes, underground passages, and the gardens that George and his wife, Olivia, had lovingly tended themselves. This was George's sanctuary, he said, the place where he felt most at peace.

They sat down for tea, and George told Guy that he had attended several Cirque du Soleil shows and loved them. "I admire what you have done, and it seems like we have a lot in common when it comes to creativity." He paused. "I know I am dying. I don't know how many years I have left, but before I go, I'd like to do a creative project with the Beatles' music. Do you think Cirque would like to be involved?"

It was the type of question that needed no answer. Guy knew how famously protective the Beatles have always been about their legacy. In the more than thirty years since the band had broken up, its recorded music and images had never been authorized for use in a live show despite offers from the biggest entertainment companies in the world. *Of course* Guy was interested.

It wasn't until the following year, after I had started at Cirque, that discussions with the Beatles began in earnest. By then, I was fully appreciative of the magic of Guy's parties—and how he managed to turn the dull rituals of business networking into such a magnificent event that brought us to the doorstep of one of the greatest musical groups of the twentieth century. In that context, our $1 million investment was a bargain.

FIND YOUR LEVERAGE AND USE IT

I was brought into the intricate process of creating a show with the Beatles soon after Guy got a call from George saying, "The Boys will be in London next week." By that, he meant not only Paul and Ringo, but the spirit of John Lennon as represented by his widow, Yoko Ono. George had been trying for months to get the group together with Guy to discuss his idea—a nearly impossible task after the painful breakup of the Beatles and John's death in 1980. "If The Boys are in a good mood," George said, "I'll invite you over, and we all can talk about doing something together. If not, we'll just go out for a beer."

At that moment, I was learning another aspect of the creative process: how vague it can seem at first, and how slim the odds of success can appear. Normally, I would not fly all the way to another country to maybe have a beer with a potential business partner. But everything in my life was different now, and I felt giddy about this adventure. Soon, Guy and I were headed for London not knowing whether we would be having the meeting of a lifetime or hanging out with George Harrison. Either way, it sounded like a fun ride.

We flew in Guy's spacious private jet, accompanied by Gilles Ste-Croix, the Cirque cofounder who would be deeply involved if we ever got this show off the ground, and several other company executives. Franco Dragone, who was still open to directing shows for Cirque, had arranged to meet us in London to explore the project. We all seemed to agree that now that we had our foot in the door, we must do everything we could to push that door open!

Normally, on a transatlantic flight like this, we would have some food and a glass of wine and get some rest. But we were all too excited to sleep. We debated for hours how we should present ourselves to the Beatles—if, in fact, the meeting ever took place. What would they be like? What should we say? What worried us most was whether the chemistry would be right. Some at Cirque were against the whole idea of working with the Beatles, mostly because we had never devoted an entire show to the work of another artist. They were concerned that the Beatles would want to control everything and we would lose the magic that made our shows great. Was it even possible to be respectful of their brand while making sure they were respectful of ours?

After we landed, our conversations continued in a hotel room, where we were joined by Franco. But by then, we weren't really listening to each other. Everyone was staring at the phone, waiting for the call from George.

As we waited, we knew we had already passed one important test with the Beatles. At Guy's urging, George and Olivia had brought Paul McCartney and his then fiancée, Heather Mills, to the *O* show in Las Vegas. They loved its dreamy, abstract feel and were very impressed by the creativity and talent. But Guy knew that selling them on Cirque was only half the battle. George had another motive that presented an enormous obstacle: he was looking for a way to get the Beatles to work on a creative project together again.

Finally, the phone rang. Guy answered, spoke briefly, and then hung up, shouting, "Yessss!" We jumped in a cab and hurried to the Mandarin Oriental hotel. The lobby looked like something out of a spy movie, with security guards swarming and whispering to each other through their earbud communication devices: "The Cirque du Soleil people are here."

When we entered the Beatles' hotel suite, the scene was surreal. Here I was, less than a year after starting my job, nervous as a schoolboy and face-to-face with the three surviving Beatles, who each approached us to shake hands—Paul McCartney, Ringo Starr, and George Harrison. And there was Yoko Ono and Olivia Harrison. It was overwhelming. I never dreamed I'd *ever* be in a business meeting like this.

As the initiator of this event, George began introducing us. Each person was pretty much as you might imagine. As all Beatles fans know, there was a clear hierarchy in the band, especially in the early years—John, followed by Paul, then George, and lastly Ringo. With John gone, Paul was in charge, something you could feel as soon as he was introduced. A true people pleaser, Paul wants everyone to feel good. *No wonder he's such a star!* I thought. He began flattering us effusively, telling us how much he loved our shows and how creative we were, talking over everyone else, one compliment after another. Naturally, we all fell in love with Paul.

George, "the quiet Beatle," was very down-to-earth, like your next-door neighbor. When the band broke up, he tried his best to have a normal life. And that's the way he handled the room that day—an average guy, just like everybody else. And Ringo was being Ringo: hanging back at first, but then cracking jokes, one after another. He was relaxed and easygoing, always deferential to Paul. As I noticed later, when Paul is happy, Ringo is happy.

Olivia was there because George had been ill and needed her assistance. She was quite outspoken, more than anyone except Paul, talking about the Cirque shows she had seen and being very charming. The quietest of all was Yoko. She only talked a little, in her quiet voice, about the artistry of Cirque, and how much John would have liked to be involved in this project. For the most part, she stayed silent. Despite the freighted history between Yoko and the surviving Beatles, I saw no outward signs of tension.

I was told, incredibly, that this may have been the first time this group had all gathered for a business meeting since John's death. As stakeholders in the Beatles legacy, they did have to interact from time to time to make decisions. But the process was never easy. Neil Aspinall, CEO of the band's management company, Apple Corps, once explained the group's organizing principle this way: "It's sort of like an inverted democracy. If one person doesn't want to do something, we don't do it. It's not like three can overrule one."

With that history as background, we wrapped up the small talk and Ringo cut to the chase: "Okay, so what's the pitch?"

Guy did not miss a beat. "There is no pitch!" he said. "You are a creative force; we are a creative force. Let's just find a way to create a show together."

There was silence for a moment, and I could immediately see this was a brilliant maneuver. With one stroke, Guy had placed Cirque on the same creative level as the Beatles. Rather than dreaming up something in advance and hoping to win their approval, he simply offered to join together as equal partners to create something magical. In any business negotiation, it's important to recognize what leverage you have and to use it. In this case, our leverage was our reputation for supreme creativity. We did not want to merely license the Beatles' brand and let them call the shots. Right away, before we invested any time and money in this project, Guy wanted them to understand that this would have to be a shared creative process. If they could not accept that, we were prepared to walk away.

TRUST THE CREATIVE PROCESS

It was immediately clear that Guy's appeal to the Beatles' innate artistic curiosity, hoping a blank canvas would draw them in, was a wise move.

Ringo turned to Paul, looking impressed, and said, "That's quite a change!"

Paul began drawing a picture of the Nowhere Man on a piece of paper. Giving the drawing to Guy, he said, "When you guys figure out what this means and can do a show with it, I'm in!"

Nobody was sure exactly what that meant, but we took it as an encouraging sign. By the time we shook hands and parted ways, I think we all knew it was about as successful as a first meeting could possibly be: all four Beatles stakeholders agreed that we should get in touch with Neil Aspinall at Apple Corps to explore the idea further.

That's when my long journey of negotiating with the Beatles began. I would spend the next two years in complex talks with Neil, working side by side with our chief financial officer, Robert Blain, trying to reach a historic agreement.

During this first meeting, the Beatles seemed to intuitively understand the importance of not defining a project before it has been explored deeply. They knew how to trust the uncertain, messy, sometimes frustrating creative process—trust the Magical Mystery Tour, you might say. "We've always liked to associate ourselves with slightly crazy people," Paul said later. "Because *we* are slightly crazy. Artists are slightly crazy. So, to work with Cirque, we were drawing on that same attraction."

When we returned from London, everyone at Cirque was excited, our minds racing with possibilities. Not long afterward, tragedy struck. George underwent an operation to remove a cancerous growth from one of his lungs. Later, he was treated for a brain tumor. He began radiation treatments, but it was too late. In Los Angeles in November of 2001, George met with Paul and Ringo for the last time, spending hours together laughing and remembering old times. On November 29, he died at the age of fifty-eight.

Guy was devastated by the news—and so was I, though I did not know George nearly as well. I felt blessed to be invited to attend his funeral, a small, modest affair, and was struck by Olivia's great strength despite her crushing sadness. (Paul and Ringo were not there to keep the crowds and paparazzi from spiraling out of control.) I also attended the Concert for George at the Royal Albert Hall in London, with musical direction by Eric Clapton, which was extremely moving.

EMOTION CAN DRIVE A PROJECT FORWARD

With George gone, Guy and I assumed the Beatles venture was over. It had been George's idea, after all. He was the main driver, the one who had somehow brought Yoko and The Boys back together, if briefly. But in the months following his death, something miraculous happened. Yoko and Paul and Ringo realized they wanted to do it more than ever, to make George's dream come true. Olivia, who had always strongly supported the project, saw it as an important way to continue her late husband's legacy.

"I think George's dying wish to his fellow Beatles was, 'Let's do something with Cirque; let's roll the dice and see where it goes,'" Jonathan Clyde, a producer for Apple Corps, told me. Jonathan knew George well, having run his Dark Horse Records label in the early 1970s. "George's feeling was simply, 'Cirque is a brilliant theatrical producer and they have great imagination, so why not try combining that with the Beatles music? It could be an amazing show.'"

That moment made me realize how powerful emotion can be when trying to push a worthy project forward. Whether the field is sports, the arts, or even one's own personal ambition, finding the emotional heartbeat beneath any venture can unleash strong currents of energy that can make the difference between success and failure.

With all the major stakeholders on board, the next phase of the project began: the business negotiations. The toughest part was how to negotiate with people who don't need the money. Most deals I've worked on throughout my career eventually came down to haggling over dollar signs, so this was a whole new experience. We were discussing art, not money, our main issue being, "How can we reassure the Beatles that we will not damage their profound legacy?"

Clearly, I could not act like a salesman trying to seduce the Beatles. And I was in no position to cajole or bully them, which is not my style anyway. Instead, I had to put my faith in the creative process that started the moment Paul McCartney handed us his drawing of the Nowhere Man. Even though we were all flying blind, we had to have faith that the Beatles and Cirque would find a way to work productively together.

"I think the biggest challenge, for both Cirque and Apple, was that both of us are very independent, successful, and I would even say arrogant," Jonathan told me later, with a chuckle. There were also big cultural differences: the British businesspeople at Apple were reserved and did not enjoy conflict, whereas Cirque's French Canadians were much more flamboyant and passionate. And we approached the project from diametrically opposite viewpoints: Cirque tends to think of the visual aspect of a show first, then the music. For the Beatles, naturally, it was the other way around.

DON'T FORCE YOUR VISION ON PARTNERS

Given all that, it's not surprising that fireworks erupted at the very first meeting between Apple and Cirque in Montreal in early 2002. The night before we met, I hosted a dinner at my house. We all had a lovely time. As everyone was leaving, I gave our guests a CD prepared by our creative team. Until then, Cirque had always used live musicians in our shows, so we just assumed there would be musicians onstage. To give them an idea of what the music might sound like, we went into a studio and played around with some Beatles recordings, adding vocals by some Montreal musicians and singers and splicing in beats the way a club DJ might do to make the tracks feel more contemporary.

That was a big mistake.

At the meeting the next day, the Apple side, in their usual restrained manner, made it clear they were deeply unhappy after listening to the CD. Cirque clearly had no understanding or appreciation of the Beatles' music, they said, and it was hard to imagine how we could ever work together. (I was glad it didn't come up that Guy, growing up in the 1970s and '80s, had always been more of a fan of Led Zeppelin and Deep Purple than the Beatles!) Our visitors had no interest in doing a tribute show— hundreds of bands were already doing that.

"Without question, we *have* to use the original recordings," said Aspinall.

"What do you mean?" Gilles Ste-Croix replied. "Play CDs?"

"Not exactly."

"Well, how exactly do you intend to use the original recordings?"

Aspinall shrugged. "We don't really know."

We were stuck, and tensions were high. The Apple team considered our CD arrogant and presumptuous—like we were dictating to them what the show should sound like. Putting myself in their shoes, I could only imagine our reaction if Apple had told us how to stage the acrobatics! We seemed to have forgotten the lesson of our first meeting with The Boys: early pitches that are too specific can stifle creativity. We forgot that we were engaging in an open-ended collaboration between equals.

We had blown our chances of working with the Beatles before the project had even gotten off the ground! That's how it appeared, at least. Fortunately, our lines of communication remained open, and Guy and I had time to talk things over. Since neither side had done anything like this before, we had no road map to follow. Our problem seemed insurmountable: we wanted to create a show with the Beatles, but they clearly did not trust us with their music.

What to do? We could have tried to convince them to trust us, but that seemed doomed to fail. Instead, we began asking a different question: Who *would* they trust?

SEARCH FOR CREATIVE SOLUTIONS
TO BREAK DEADLOCKS

I'm not sure who spoke the name first, but eventually Guy and I came up with the only possible answer: George Martin.

In Beatles lore, Martin has always been called the Fifth Beatle for good reason: as an extraordinary arranger, musician, composer, and engineer, he was an integral part of the band's success from the beginning (along with their manager, Brian Epstein). Why not ask Martin to take charge of the music and let Cirque focus on the rest of the show?

Immediately, I called Aspinall, who liked the idea so much I could feel his sense of relief. We had been at a dead end, and here was an intriguing solution. Until then, he thought we wanted to control the music, but our proposal was convincing him otherwise. This is an important point when it comes to negotiating: When you are deadlocked, look for a creative way out. Make the other side feel you genuinely understand their position, and try to accommodate them. Too many people equate this sort of accommodation with weakness or failure. They always want to be right and to not give an inch. That is so wrongheaded. If you can come up with a solution that satisfies the other party but doesn't hurt you, why not try it? Even if the idea doesn't work, it breeds trust that can lead to a breakthrough down the road.

RESPECT AND TRUST
YOUR PARTNER'S EXPERTISE

As soon as we hung up, Neil called George Martin, who was very interested except for one problem: at age seventy-six, he was losing his hearing and felt he could not do the job without help. He suggested his son Giles Martin, then in his early thirties. A successful producer in his own right, having worked with artists such as Elvis Costello and INXS, Giles jumped at the chance to work with his father and use the latest technology to unpack those famous recordings and see how they might be reengineered for a Cirque show.

That was the breakthrough we needed. Now we had a framework and a process: both sides would consult with the other, but when disagreements arose, the Beatles would have the final say on the music and Cirque would have the final word on the visual show. That was a revelation for me. When beginning any creative partnership, it's crucial to respect and trust each other's expertise. Each side must be free to pursue their vision without feeling they are being controlled or manipulated by the other side.

Immediately, our tensions with Apple evaporated. Now that the Beatles were confident the music was in good hands, we became a unified team chasing the same goal: creating a spectacular, deeply felt celebration of the band and its music. More than anything, the Cirque team wanted to impress the Beatles, which of course included Yoko and Olivia as surrogates for John and George. There would be no point in doing a show with the Beatles if the Beatles themselves didn't like it. Guy and Gilles and I became obsessed with making sure that we produced a true work of art that everyone would be proud of.

STAY HUMBLE AND REMAIN PATIENT

In the end, we needed every ounce of that enthusiasm to keep the project going. This was one of the most complex transactions I have ever negotiated. Not only did we have to satisfy the Beatles and Apple, but nothing could happen without the approval of the two companies that owned the rights to the Beatles music—Sony for song publishing and EMI for the actual recordings. Apple had assured us that getting the necessary rights would not be a problem. That was turning out *not* to be the case, and it was a hugely frustrating problem. Eventually, Apple would make a deal with Sony, but EMI was another story. After years of contract disputes and court battles, EMI and Apple had a contentious relationship. Talks stalled as EMI imposed one condition after another, eventually making the project too costly to be feasible.

This was maddening. How were we supposed to create a show when we didn't even know for sure that we could use the music? It was one of many times Guy and I said, "Fuck it. We don't need this aggravation." But each time, we realized we could not give up. This could be not only one of the biggest shows in Cirque's history, but a cultural landmark celebrating one of the most famous bands in the world. We *had* to keep trying.

To make matters worse, Franco Dragone had dropped out as director. He wanted his own company to coproduce the show, but that was a nonstarter for us (Cirque has always produced its own shows). Despite all the uncertainties, we knew we had to move ahead with choosing a new director. It was quite a challenge. We needed someone with a powerful, original vision, obsessed with what I like to call "the urgency to create," who could also navigate the emotional minefields that came with the territory. Accommodating the viewpoints of such a diverse cast of characters—from Apple, the Beatles, and Cirque—would not be easy.

After some deliberation, we settled on Dominic Champagne, who had already directed our successful touring show *Varekai* and rescued *Zumanity*. Great under pressure, diplomatic, good-hearted, and someone we trusted completely, Dominic was an ideal fit. After *Zumanity*'s opening in September of 2003, Guy popped the question on his private jet as they flew back to Montreal. Negotiations between Apple and the record companies were continuing, Guy said, but we needed a director to start sketching out ideas for the show. A huge Beatles fan, Dominic was awestruck. "For months," he told me later, "I could not believe that I was the one."

Dominic dove into his work at about the same time as George and Giles Martin began theirs. Immediately, they started discussing the overwhelming task of how to choose which of the hundreds of Beatles recordings to include in the ninety-minute show. They would have to strike a balance between songs by John, Paul, and George (and probably one by Ringo), songs from the early days to the later years, and songs that cover a wide range of styles and feeling. It could not be simply a greatest-hits compilation, they decided—it would probably include more obscure songs as well. The only thing they knew for sure was that no matter what they decided, they would catch hell from Beatles fans.

Visiting the historic Abbey Road Studios in London, the father-and-son team began delicately excavating the priceless original masters of the band's recordings, which the elder Martin called, only half-jokingly, the Holy Grail. Eventually, George and Giles put together a fifteen-minute demo that showcased the approach they proposed to take. For one track, they took Ringo's drum solo from *Abbey Road*'s "The End"—the only drum solo he ever recorded with the Beatles—and placed it at the beginning of "Get Back," along with sounds of cheering crowds. On another track, they layered together "Tomorrow Never Knows" (from *Revolver*) and "Within You Without You" (from *Sgt. Pepper's Lonely Hearts Club Band*).

Paul and Ringo had given the Martins carte blanche to go wherever their ears led them. Still, young Giles was especially nervous before playing the demo for them. "We said to them, try to be as experimental as you can," Paul said later. "So they gave us this little demo playback, and suddenly they'd taken 'Within You Without You,' put the 'Tomorrow Never Knows' drums on it, and then started to bring in guitar from here and a thing from there, and we went, 'That's it, exactly. That's what we're talking about.' And I think we were all amazed how well it worked."

George Martin became a steadying presence, making me realize how important it is to have a wise elder when engaged in a creative process that's so open ended. With his deep under-standing of each of the four Beatles and their music, he pro-vided the compass everyone needed to navigate these uncharted waters. He was the consummate gentleman, gracefully manag-ing everyone's needs—including my own. My craving was for stories about the Beatles. I loved listening to them as a boy as I sat at my desk doing homework. I'm sure I drove George quite crazy with my endless questions, but he handled them all gracefully. When I visited Abbey Road Studios to listen to the Martins' demo, I was awestruck, my bliss heightened when George began describing the time he brought in a symphony orchestra to record "Yesterday."

As the father-and-son team worked on the music, Dominic began confiding in George about how intimidated he felt by the whole assignment and how haunted he was by the ghosts of the two departed Beatles. While doing his research, he found an interview in which John Lennon said he never wanted to end up like so many pop stars, singing his greatest hits in Las Vegas. Could Dominic construct a Vegas show that John would actually be proud of, not embarrassed by? In an early acoustic version of "While My Guitar Gently Weeps," when he heard George Har-rison singing, "I look from the wings at the play you are staging," the director said he could almost feel George's gaze upon him.

As Dominic told me later, "You don't want to be the one who is given a $100 million budget, the incredible Beatles universe of poetry and music, and the talent of Cirque du Soleil, and spoil the party."

"So what kind of a show is it going to be?" George Martin asked.

"It won't be an opera, that's for sure," Dominic replied. "It won't be a rock show, it's not a musical, and it's not a play."

"Okay, so what is it?"

Dominic thought some more. "You know what?" he finally said. "Let's make a rock 'n' roll poem."

That became Dominic's guiding principle, the lens through which he saw the show. Everything would be in the service of creating a rock 'n' roll poem. Working with director of creation Gilles Ste-Croix (acting essentially as producer), Dominic came up with some guidelines. They would not have actors portraying the Beatles onstage or dwell on the biographical details of the band. That would be far too literal and predictable. Rather, they wanted to evoke the essence of the band and its music mostly by mining the rich trove of characters and stories and the emotions and imagery from the songs themselves—Eleanor Rigby, Lady Madonna, Lucy in the Sky with Diamonds, Strawberry Fields, the Nowhere Man, Sgt. Pepper, the Octopus's Garden, and more.

This would not be easy. Our team was attempting to create visual representations of music that people all over the world knew by heart and had already imbued with their own meanings and images. That is the beauty of art, of course—it can mean so many different things to different people—but that very flexibility makes any attempt at interpretation exceedingly difficult. Perhaps most intimidating, the Beatles themselves had to recognize their songs, feel their own inspiration in creating them, and see themselves as they watched the show.

To extract the deepest meaning from each song, Dominic and Gilles studied the historical record and met separately with Paul, Ringo, Olivia Harrison, and Yoko Ono. They conducted a tour of Liverpool, where the band began; the club in Hamburg, Germany, where they played their legendary marathon early gigs; the famous Abbey Road recording studio; and the rooftop of the Apple building on London's Savile Row, where they played in public for the last time.

Dominic had not worked on the project long when we informed him that—assuming we were able to obtain the music rights—the show would have to open in December of 2005, sooner than expected. We were teaming up once again with MGM Resorts International, with whom we had an exclusive contract to host all of our Las Vegas resident shows. (It would be our fifth production together after *Mystère*, *O*, *Zumanity*, and *KÀ*.) At the time, MGM was reeling from a horrific accident that became international news: during the Siegfried & Roy magic show at the Mirage resort, performer Roy Horn was bitten on the neck and dragged offstage by a 400-pound white tiger.

That show closed immediately, and the Mirage theater remained vacant for months, putting MGM under tremendous pressure to install a new show as quickly as possible. It really wanted the Beatles production and was willing to wait, but not forever. For every month the theater was empty, MGM was losing $5 million.

Dominic objected to the new deadline, arguing that there was not enough time to do the show properly. At one point, he even threatened to quit. Fortunately, the crisis was solved later when our creative team got the idea I described earlier in the book: they wanted to renovate the Mirage space as a theater-in-the-round, with audience members sitting in a 360-degree circle around the stage. That would add another six months to the theater-renovation process, pushing the opening date to June of 2006. Now Dominic had the time he needed to put the show together.

But as the development process continued, we still didn't have the rights to the Beatles music. As Apple's negotiations with EMI dragged on, with no end in sight, Neil Aspinall delivered some bad news: he might not be able to obtain the music rights to the show after all.

Guy and I were furious. Neil had assured us, time and again, that he would get the rights. Now, after we had invested so much time, money, and energy, the whole project was apparently dead. Frustrated, Guy and I had little choice but to tell Bobby Baldwin, the Mirage Resorts CEO, that we may not be able to produce a Beatles show after all.

"Guys, if you can't deliver the Beatles," he snapped, throwing in a few colorful adjectives, clearly agitated, "just give me a Cirque du Soleil show!" That's when Guy and I decided we needed a plan B. We immediately began preparing another production as a substitute, but it was a half-hearted effort at best. By then, everybody at Cirque had our hearts set on the Beatles.

At our wits' end, Neil and I came up with one last, desperate plan. I would write a letter to Apple saying we are so sorry that we won't be able to stage this show because, based on our past successes in Las Vegas, it would generate millions of dollars per year for Apple over a period of at least ten years. Aspinall would then show the letter to EMI executives and threaten to sue them to recover those millions. This was no empty threat. Neil was 100 percent ready to go to court.

I wrote the letter, and Neil passed it on. We waited. Incredibly, the plan worked, and Apple Corps did not have to sue. In the summer of 2004, EMI came around and made a deal.

The process of getting the Beatles show to this point contained many important lessons. First, if you threaten to sue a partner as Neil did, you must be ready to follow through. Otherwise, the partner could call your bluff and never believe you again if you try to get tough.

More importantly, these events remind me how often businesspeople stay away from projects that have too many unanswered questions, unexpected snags, and murky prospects for success. They want solid guarantees and predictable outcomes. I was like that, too, in my pre-Cirque days. But I have learned that living a creative life provides few such assurances. You must get used to uncomfortable feelings of doubt and uncertainty, knowing they are part of the process.

I'm not advocating wearing blinders. Sometimes, when a project is not working, you have to bail out. Maybe it has become too costly or distracts you from other important business. If that's the case, by all means cut and run. But it's important to be honest about your motives. Can you really not afford to stay the course, or has your patience simply run out? Which is suffering the most—your bottom line, or your ego and pride?

So many times, Guy and I were tempted to pull the plug on the Beatles show. In every instance, we tried to stay humble and remain patient. We knew the day was coming when we would not have enough time to create the show the Beatles deserved and would have to shift gears to plan B. Until that happened, we kept going, powered by a clear-eyed understanding that, despite endless frustration, success was still possible as long as we kept our eyes on the prize.

MOBILIZE PEOPLE AROUND YOUR PROJECT

Once our contracts with Apple were signed, we faced the daunting task of actually creating a show that lived up to our sky-high
expectations.

Though our creative team had plenty of resources at its
disposal—our world-class performers, the latest technology,
deep experience creating hit shows—we also had an unusual
set of constraints. This time, we had to please all the Beatles
stakeholders. Though we had final say on all visual aspects of the
production, we desperately wanted to please Paul, Ringo, Yoko,
and Olivia. So we went to great lengths to regularly solicit input
from all of them.

Fortunately, we did not see this as an intrusion on our process
but a fundamental part of it that would make the show stronger
and deeper. Every business has similar constituencies to satisfy—
customers, government regulators, shareholders, suppliers, and
others. Learning how their concerns can improve the product is
a crucial part of trusting the creative process.

For the Beatles show, the musical team (George and Giles
Martin) and the visual team (primarily Dominic and Gilles)
would periodically visit with each of the Beatles stakeholders
to show them how their part of the show was progressing—
everything from music and band images to costumes and
choreography—and then listen carefully to the responses. (In
keeping with his laid-back, accommodating personality, Ringo
felt less of a need to be deeply involved.)

At first, Paul thought we were too evasive about our plans.
"They'd say, 'Don't worry, it's going to be great.' And I'd say,
'But what are you going to hang it on?' Then they came up with
this idea that the show is based on—[acts performed early in the

show] with ladders, and buildings going up after World War II, Eleanor Rigby coming through. And I felt, okay, that's enough, that's all I needed."

By the fall of 2005, the planning stage was over. We had developed the concept, sketched out the acts, made the costumes, and assembled a team of performers. Now it was time to start rehearsing and refining the show at our studios in Montreal. There were acts on trapeze, aerial Russian swing, trampoline, bungees, skates, and lots of dancers—more than usual for a Cirque show. Eventually, more than 120 Beatles songs would be sampled to create 40 musical pieces. Since many of the songs were not long enough to last for an entire act, they were combined with other songs in startling, innovative ways to create a powerful mash-up. In one case, George Martin wrote a beautiful string arrangement to accompany a studio demo of George Harrison's "While My Guitar Gently Weeps."

Watching the show take shape, I was struck by how long and difficult the process was. We tend to think that artists merely execute some visionary idea that arrives out of the blue, fully formed. In reality, it's often a cumbersome, awkward string of failures that may or may not eventually lead to discovery. Just look at the songwriting partnership of Lennon and McCartney to see how they bounced unfinished ideas off each other to weed out what didn't work and refine and develop what did. (John, especially, was rarely happy with the final recorded version.)

Even an experienced and decorated artist like Dominic had to be reminded of the importance of failure as he worked. "You tend to feel that because you have the Beatles on one hand and Cirque du Soleil on the other that you cannot fail," he told me. "But a creative process is a huge number of failures until you find what works. It took me a while before I could say, 'Okay, I don't have to be a genius bringing a masterpiece every morning. I just need to make a show like every other show I've done, I'm sure that when Lennon made his first demo of 'Strawberry Fields Forever,' it was not a masterpiece."

After a few months, Olivia and Yoko came to Montreal to watch rehearsals for the first time. While Paul and Ringo were happy to give their fellow artists at Cirque plenty of creative freedom to interpret their songs, the two widows had a much different mission—protecting the legacy of their late husbands—and were not nearly as acquiescent. In fact, if you eavesdropped on their conversations with Dominic and Gilles during their visit, you got a sense of the huge challenge they *all* faced trying to be polite and accommodating while also giving their sometimes blunt and emotional opinions about what they were watching onstage.

"I feel strongly about the two characters from the beginning of the show," Olivia told Dominic during a break. She shifted uncomfortably in her seat as performers milled about the stage in front of her. "Can I speak freely?"

Dominic nodded.

"I don't particularly *like* those characters. I don't know if it was, you know—"

Yoko cut in, nodding in agreement. "In the beginning, he was in *too much*."

Dominic tried to explain that those characters emerged from the songs, which were chosen to make sure each Beatle was represented fairly according to his songwriting contributions to the band. So far, he said, the show had fourteen songs by John, thirteen by Paul, four by George, and one by Ringo. Art, I was realizing, is far more collaborative than I imagined.

DON'T LET CRITICISM STIFLE
THE CREATIVE PROCESS

By early 2006, renovations at the Mirage in Las Vegas were far enough along that we could move rehearsals into the theater. At this point in a show's development, all the acts are somewhat hypothetical until we can see how well they work in the actual space where the production will take place. Moving was a huge undertaking. We transported truckloads of gear, a crew of nearly one hundred technicians, and a cast of sixty talented performers from all over the world.

When the production arrived in Vegas, it was an exciting, nerve-racking moment. The show—now titled *The Beatles LOVE*—was starting to feel real.

Two months later, on a warm day in April, a buzz swept through the Mirage theater. A VIP would be visiting to see how the show was progressing: Sir Paul McCartney.

"It would be enormously helpful if you could show him as much of the show as possible," George Martin told Dominic before Paul arrived. "Because he hasn't seen any of it and he's intensely curious about it."

Dominic scowled. With the premiere only two months away, technical problems were routinely producing delays that could last for hours. Even when everything was functioning properly, the show was not ready to be shown to *anybody*, let alone Paul McCartney. "Let's not put ourselves in a context where it's thumbs-up or thumbs-down," the director said. "We're not there yet. For me, it's all thumbs-down."

But it was too late. Paul was already in Vegas, on his way to the Mirage. His handlers had told us that his time was limited, so we decided to start as soon as he showed up. Not long afterward, Paul entered the theater dressed casually in a T-shirt.

"We're thrilled to have you here," Dominic said, nervously shaking Paul's hand. After an awkward pause, the director confessed, "Everybody has butterflies in their stomach."

"Good," Paul joked. "I want to keep everybody in a state of tension."

Everybody laughed and Paul took his seat. Immediately, the artists and crew launched into an acrobatic act, but Dominic wasn't happy with it. As Paul watched, the director wondered aloud whether to try to fix it or just cut the act completely. "It's never been worse than this," he sighed.

Paul did not seem to notice such flaws—or if he did, he kept his thoughts to himself. Mostly, he watched mesmerized. I was sitting in front of Paul, who was seated next to George Martin, and I could hear them talking during the Eleanor Rigby act. "For me, what's really strange about this is remembering writing these things, which was so *little*," Paul said. He scrunched his hand, pretending to write in the air with a small pencil. "Little guitar or piano music, little paper and pencil, back of an envelope [writing] 'Sgt. Pepper' or something." Then he spread his arms wide and gazed up in wonder at the $100 million theater with high ceilings, elaborate rigging, and trapeze artists in wild costumes flying through space. "And look what's happened to it!"

Watching Paul throughout the day reminded me that leadership does not always require criticism, which can stifle the creative process. As a musician, he understands that what other artists often need, more than anything, is encouragement.

"I *love* the shadow sequence," he told Dominic after watching four silhouetted figures run around comically as recordings of the Beatles' actual voices filled the theater. "This is something to be *not* nervous about. It's really good."

Dominic looked grateful but uneasy. "I'm sorry for the rest."

"Come on, man, we understand," Paul said, like a reassuring older brother. "You know, we've been at this a long time too."

There were many delays that day, common during our rehearsals. With every pause in the action, someone from Paul's entourage came over to see if he still wanted to stay. "Are you kidding?" he said at one point. "This is our show!" That's when I breathed a sigh of relief. Neil Aspinall had told me, during his visit, "If Paul says it's *our* show, we are in business!"

After the rehearsal, Paul addressed the whole cast and crew: "We just watched a little bit, and we think it's fantastic, really exciting." As everyone applauded, he joked, "But I want you to work harder! Much harder!" The room erupted in laughter. Afterward, he invited some of us out for dinner. At the restaurant, I was so excited that I couldn't stop asking him questions about the Beatles. Their best times, he said, were the days they spent in the studio. "That's what we enjoyed the most," he said, "writing and recording new songs." That day with Paul was among my most cherished memories of the whole adventure.

ALL YOU NEED IS LOVE

When *The Beatles LOVE* finally premiered at the Mirage in June of 2006, it was an emotional Beatles reunion. The paparazzi were there to catch all the famous faces as they entered the theater: Paul, Ringo, and Olivia with her son, Dhani Harrison. John was represented by Yoko and their son, Sean Lennon, as well as his first wife, Cynthia, and their son, Julian Lennon. For a moment, all of the rancor that raged when things fell apart—the Beatles as a band, John's first marriage—was forgotten.

During the show, it was clear that the two most important members of the audience loved it. Paul and Ringo, sitting together, whispered to each another excitedly, with Paul singing along and Ringo air-drumming. That said it all.

"I was surprised with the emotion I felt when I heard, like, the four voices and the songs of George and John, you know, when Paul and I are sitting next to each other," Ringo said afterward. "So, two of our brothers were in the room but they weren't sitting next to us."

Earlier, Yoko had artfully summed up the show's power: "The Beatles were like acrobats of the mind, and Cirque du Soleil are acrobats of the body. So, when they come together, it makes something that's whole. I like that." At the premiere, wearing an all-white outfit and an enormous white hat, she said, "The only regret is that John is not here because I'm sure that he would have loved it."

When the show was over, Paul, Ringo, George and Giles Martin, and the families of John and George joined Dominic, Gilles, and Guy onstage to celebrate the Beatles coming together one last time to create this spectacular production. Paul yelled, "Just one special round of applause for John and George!" and the crowd went wild.

At one point, Paul and Yoko kissed and hugged. Later, Neil Aspinall told me, "I *never* thought I would see that."

The reviews were ecstatic. "*LOVE* limns Beatles music as no production, be it for stage or film, has ever done before," said *Variety*, calling the show a "graceful and elegant marriage of movement and song that reinforces the greatness of the music created by the Beatles."

After opening night, *The Beatles LOVE* played ten times a week, exciting crowds and critics alike. At the Grammy Awards in 2008, George and Giles won two trophies for the soundtrack album. On the show's tenth anniversary, we closed the Mirage theater for three weeks while Dominic installed a $10 million refresh. Again, it drew rave reviews and boosted ticket sales, helping to make *LOVE* one of Cirque's best-selling shows. Paul, Yoko, and Olivia often returned to the Mirage theater, bringing family and friends.

One towering figure was absent during the premiere of the rebooted production in July of 2016. Sir George Martin had passed away a few months earlier at the age of ninety (at his memorial service, mourners heard "While My Guitar Gently Weeps" from the soundtrack album he created). In his absence, we were left with his words that summed up what the show meant—not just to him, but to the world: "Every generation, as it grows up, finds the Beatles for themselves. My children did, and now my grandchildren. With this show, we see how it will go on."

The Beatles LOVE had a huge impact on everyone involved. "I've been very nostalgic about the sixties, all those years of freedom and revolution," said Dominic just before the 2006 premiere, adding that he came of age during a later period that felt more cynical. Exhausted by rehearsals, his voice broke with emotion as he talked about how the show had touched him. "And I feel like today I'm back to my roots of dreaming that we can 'take a sad song and make it better,' as the man said."

Today, every time I watch the production, a flood of memories comes rushing back: Guy's wild party that inspired George Harrison to reach out to him; our first meeting with the Beatles in London; the endless negotiations; the fear of failing; and the long, pressure-filled roller-coaster ride to opening night. Sometimes I reflect on how perfect the show's title is. The creative process is often difficult, unpredictable, and maddening, just like life. But in the final number of the show, the Beatles offer the best advice about how to handle it: "All you need is love."

CHAPTER 4

SLIPPING ON A BANANA PEEL

It was during the making of *The Beatles LOVE* that my long apprenticeship under Guy Laliberté ended and I began feeling more comfortable steering the ship myself. As we negotiated with Apple Corps, Guy trusted me to take the lead and make that complex deal happen. Then, in the spring of 2006, he invited me to a breakfast meeting at his home. Over eggs and coffee, he began hinting (not very subtly) that he was ready to give up the title of chief executive officer.

It was not the first time we'd had this conversation. Since the day I was hired, Guy had been talking about spending less time on the business side and more energy on things he was passionate about—developing new shows, expanding our international reach, providing overall strategic direction, and promoting his favorite charitable cause of alleviating poverty and water shortages around the world. But on this morning, it was clear that he was prepared to finally relinquish responsibility for day-to-day operations and step back into a role he called "Cirque's founder and creative guide."

Sensing where the conversation was heading, I said simply, "I'm ready."

"Of course you are!" Guy laughed. "So let's move on it!"

FOUNDERS MUST LET GO

With that, I became CEO. From that moment on, our relationship worked beautifully because Guy gave me real authority—something many company founders have trouble doing. Having started their firms from scratch, entrepreneurs often feel they know better about every little decision and can't stop micromanaging. But Guy was true to his word. He informed employees that it wouldn't do any good complaining to him about any decisions I made because my word was final.

That also applied to people outside the company. At one meeting, a potential partner was unhappy with an answer I gave him, so he called Guy to plead his case. Guy stopped him short, saying I was the one leading the negotiations. That gave me instant credibility and stature. In other ways, large and small, Guy allowed me to do my job without interference, and I never had to worry about him looking over my shoulder.

For my part, I had to decide which issues to bring to Guy's attention and which to not bother him about. The key was keeping our lines of responsibility clear. He had zero interest in which vendor I chose for our new computer system. But he was passionate about developing new shows, and I was fully in favor of letting him control that essential part of the business. Why not? He was the expert, not me. Understanding and respecting each other's roles and talents is critical to a smooth leadership transition, especially at a creative company whose product is a direct reflection of the founder's artistic vision. We complemented each other perfectly: I had no interest in trying to replace Guy as Cirque's driving creative force, and he was glad to have someone else run the company.

KEEP LEADERSHIP CONFLICTS PRIVATE

It's amazing to think that, in all the years that we worked together, Guy and I only had one fight—and we still joke about it. Artists can be passionate, as we all know, but unchecked emotions can lead to morale problems among employees when conflicts within the leadership team spill into view.

The argument started during an executive meeting as we discussed a deal I was negotiating. Guy felt I was underselling the company and got carried away. "Oh come on—don't you understand the power of our brand?!" he yelled. As we debated the matter, Guy challenged me in a loud and aggressive way.

Afterward, he came into my office and said, "That was a really good meeting, don't you think? It's great that we can be so open with each other!"

Actually, I did *not* think it was a great meeting. Leadership, in my view, requires a consistent message so employees can feel safe knowing that their superiors are working well together, not melting down in acrimony. I was upset about the way Guy had talked to me, but I also know how to keep my cool. So I said, in my calmest voice, "Guy, we have to present a unified team if we want our employees to feel secure and stay focused."

Guy was surprised that I was making an issue of this. In his mind, he was just being his usual dramatic self. "Daniel, sometimes I like to put on a show!" he protested. After some back-and-forth, we decided that, going forward, whenever we had a difference of opinion, we would discuss it in private and come to a resolution. It worked. When disagreements arose, we freely expressed our opinions behind closed doors, respected each other's viewpoint, and never fought again.

TAKE OFF THOSE ROSE-COLORED GLASSES

As I started my new job as CEO in May of 2006, I reflected on how lucky I was to join Cirque when I did, five years earlier, just as the company was beginning an amazing period of explosive growth. Starting in 2002, we opened eight shows in six years, a breakneck pace for us. All were successful and some were mega-hits, from *KÀ*, *Zumanity*, and *The Beatles LOVE* in Las Vegas to the touring shows *Varekai*, *Corteo*, *Delirium*, *Kooza*, and *Wintuk*. By 2007, we had reached more than $600 million in revenues and felt invincible. There seemed to be no limit to how big we could get with our laser-like focus on new and existing markets for our shows.

Then everything began to fall apart. In retrospect, the culprit was a potent combination of the global financial crisis of 2008, natural disasters, and our own missteps. Cirque's Golden Age was ending, replaced by a tumultuous five-year period that became, by far, the most challenging since our crazy early days.

The Great Recession was the first disaster, turning the world on its head almost overnight. Everything we thought we could depend on was thrown into doubt, magnifying the dimensions of every other problem we encountered. This should have been a time for being grounded, cautious, and humble. But that was never the Cirque way—and by then I had fully bought into the company's daring ethos. We were a band of risk-takers with only one gear: full speed ahead. Our main response to the economic downturn was denial. We carried on as if we were somehow immune from the devastation swirling all around us.

I still wince when I look back at some of the public statements I made around this time. "All I can say is that in the past, when there was an economic crisis, people have turned to entertainment," I told one interviewer in November of 2008. "Because you just want to forget about your problems, and you're looking for hope, and you're looking for distraction, and that's entertainment. So, normally, we are not touched as bad as the other sectors of the economy."

Talk about wishful thinking! But that was our attitude. Rather than retrench and protect ourselves in the late summer and fall of 2008, we continued to expand as if nothing had changed. We developed three expensive and risky new resident shows that opened within three months of each other—one each in Las Vegas, Japan, and the Chinese island of Macao.

By this point in my life, I know that I have what some might call "selective memory." I quickly forget failures, even when I learn from them. I much prefer remembering triumphs. It's a quality that helps me remain optimistic, especially during difficult times. But failure is a great teacher, so it's worthwhile to slow down and candidly examine what went wrong during this challenging period, and why.

The first show in our losing streak was *Zaia*, a traditional Cirque acrobatic production in the mold of our iconic *Mystère*. We continued developing it and the other two shows even as the economy began showing warning signs in 2007, setting the stage for the banking crisis. With *Zaia*, our risk was compounded by the fact that we were attempting something completely new: launching the first-ever large-scale entertainment event in the Chinese gambling mecca of Macao.

Zaia opened in August of 2008 as the story of a girl's surreal trip into outer space, where she discovers a magical world of aliens. We felt it succeeded on both an artistic and entertainment level. But its fatal flaw was evident as I strolled through the resort hosting the show, the Venetian Macao.

This enormous hotel casino, so big it felt like a small city, was jammed with seventy-five thousand people gambling, but only three hundred people watched our show, in a theater with two thousand seats. Clearly, the visitors were there to gamble, not to see a show or dine at a fancy restaurant. Our attempts to transform Macao into an entertainment destination like Las Vegas—during one of the worst economic downturns in modern history—were failing badly.

STAY TRUE TO YOUR VALUES

Another big mistake we made with *Zaia* was to abandon the guidelines we always used to decide whether to embark on a new project. Informally, we called them The Four Criteria, and we still use them today. In order of importance, they are:

1. Is it a creative challenge?
2. Do our partners share our values?
3. Can we make a profit?
4. Are our partners socially engaged?

In our most successful shows, the answer to each question has been a resounding "Yes!" These rules can apply to any company, in any industry. Let's break down the list and examine each one.

1. Is It a Creative Challenge? This comes first because it's by far the most important, even for companies not in the arts or entertainment. With each new proposal, ask yourself whether your teams can get truly excited to work on the project. Employee engagement is a big problem for many companies, and it's easy to see why: managers do not give workers enough reasons to get psyched up about their jobs. No matter what field you are in, a creatively challenged staff will show up for work inspired and ready to be productive. They will even work longer hours. This is especially true for younger workers who, in survey after survey, have indicated they want their jobs to have meaning. Becoming known as a creative workplace, in turn, will help your company attract the most innovative and dynamic talent.

Another reason to make creative challenge your top priority: if you don't, you will be wearing blinders, unable to see the future of your industry. Unless you take the time to reflect about how your organization can meet the needs of customers going forward, you will never become a leader in your field—and you'll run the great risk that a nimbler competitor will come out of nowhere to beat you. Think of the way Kodak failed to realize that the digital revolution would destroy its film business. Or how Blockbuster seemed to believe people would rent movies on physical media forever. *Creativity* may seem like a trendy word or an optional component in your company's culture. The truth is quite the opposite: today, it's essential for survival.

At Cirque, we have always instinctively known that our goal of developing a spectacular show won't happen unless we get our creative juices flowing. With productions like *KÀ* or *The Beatles LOVE*, there was no question that this first criterion was being met. *Zaia*, however, was a mixed bag. It was fun and well executed, but it did not pose the same creative challenges as our more adventurous productions. That helped diminish the impact we could have made in Macao.

2. Does Our Partner Share Our Values? Up until this moment, our greatest business partner by far was MGM Resorts International, which always supported us no matter how far-out our show ideas were or how expensive the theater construction became. That's because its executives—John Redmond, Bobby Baldwin, Jim Murren, Bill Hornbuckle, and others—understood the value of art and its commercial potential. Bringing in our cutting-edge, sophisticated acts, they knew, gave their resorts the kind of upscale buzz they needed to become must-see destinations for tourists from around the world. During negotiations, they were unfailingly genuine, respectful, and helpful. More recently, our partnership with the Walt Disney Company has been tremendously satisfying and productive because we share the same beliefs about the value of art and entertainment. This principle may seem like common sense, but I'm always surprised how often companies ignore it—especially when they are seduced by the prospect of making a lot of money.

With *Zaia*, we found out what a mistake it can be to violate this rule. Though our arrangement with MGM was exclusive in Las Vegas, we were free to partner with other resorts elsewhere. In Macao, we teamed up with Sands China, and it was the first time we had worked with a different casino operator. But, as we discovered too late, that company had absolutely no interest in the artistic content or quality of our shows. Needing cultural content to obtain a gambling license, it viewed our arrangement as strictly a means to an end. As long as its casinos were full, our new partner didn't seem to care what we put up onstage for ninety minutes and did not provide the marketing support we needed to attract ticket buyers. With the values of our two companies completely out of alignment, we had one conflict after another.

3. Can It Make a Profit? For *Zaia*, the answer was a resounding "Yes!" But that was also the problem. We put this criterion third on the list for a good reason. Though profitability is obviously required, it's not something we consider until conditions #1 and #2 have been met. For *Zaia*, our priorities were backward; the profit potential became the engine that drove the project, and it's easy to see why. This was a fantastic deal for us. Sands China knew it would make huge profits by stuffing its giant casino with those seventy-five thousand gamblers playing blackjack, poker, and roulette. So it could afford to cover our entire $40 million cost of creating *Zaia*, spend another $100 million constructing the theater to house it, and guarantee us a profit for three years, no matter how many people bought tickets. It would have been difficult to turn down an incredible deal like that, but that's exactly what we should have done—not for some abstract principle but for the very practical reason that our company has never been driven by a lust for money. We are motivated by the need to create something beautiful, astonishing, inspiring—not by the prospect of riches. When we have that spark of creativity, the profits take care of themselves. Without it, we're toast.

4. Are Our Partners Socially Engaged? In discussions with new associates, we always ask about their involvement in social issues. If they are not actively engaged, we introduce them to some of our favorite causes. These include Cirque du Monde, our non-profit arm that uses circus arts to help at-risk youth, and Guy's One Drop Foundation that provides healthy drinking water to underprivileged nations around the world. At some meetings, I get blank stares when I mention this requirement, but we insist upon it. Once our new partners get involved, they are usually glad they did.

After *Zaia* opened and attracted sparse crowds, we tinkered with the show, adding touches from Chinese culture like acrobats in lion costumes and a flying dragon. But we could not fix the underlying business problems, especially in the teeth of a global recession. When our contract was up, our partner wanted to keep the show running. But playing to a nearly empty theater every night was not only demoralizing for our employees, it was damaging to our brand, which is synonymous with sold-out houses. Realizing that we had completely misjudged the market for entertainment in Macao, we closed the show in February of 2012 after a three-and-a-half-year run. We were disappointed, but glad to finally put that episode behind us.

MANAGE YOUR ENTHUSIASM

In the years before the financial crisis hit, we were developing two other resident shows besides *Zaia*: *Zed* at Tokyo Disney (based on a tarot card theme) and *Criss Angel Believe* in Las Vegas (a hybrid magic show with music and dancing). Both opened in October of 2008, just a few weeks after the collapse of Lehman Brothers on September 15 that triggered the global banking meltdown.

It's fair to wonder why we continued with our ambitious plan to open three resident shows in three months as the economy deteriorated and then fell off a cliff. I have often asked myself that same question. The best answer I can give is that we were addicted to the high of producing shows. That's what we get truly excited about, even when the more sensible course is to slow down or stop. Managing enthusiasm is one of the great challenges for a creative company. Passion is great—a prerequisite for true creativity—but it must be handled carefully to keep your company from overextending itself.

In a sign of how fully I had absorbed Cirque's effusive spirit, I was gung ho about all these projects and supported them 100 percent. Even today, it's difficult for me to feel like I'm doing my job and fulfilling my life's mission unless I'm helping to get as many thrilling new projects off the ground as possible.

Of the three shows we opened in 2008, the one that was most deserving of our attention was *Zed* in Tokyo. Had we limited ourselves to that show only, we probably would have been fine. The title character was The Fool from tarot cards who embarks on a quest to unite two mythical groups, the people of the earth and the people of the sky. It was a stunning show featuring women spinning off a trapeze with bungee cords, a high-wire act, jugglers tossing clubs of fire, a world-champion baton twirler, Chinese lasso performers, and much more. Cirque has always been huge in Japan—Tokyo and Osaka are our top two markets after Las Vegas—and once again our loyal fans there came out in great numbers to see our new show.

Alas, we did not have the internal discipline to stop there.

STICK TO YOUR CORE BUSINESS

If we were to consciously take the risk of overextending ourselves with multiple new shows, it would have made sense to stick with what we do best: ensemble acts heavy on acrobatics. Instead, we did the opposite with our third production of 2008, teaming up with a headlining magician, Criss Angel, on a show with barely any acrobatics. Today, with the benefit of hindsight, it's easy to see that this was a recipe for failure. But the success of *The Beatles LOVE* had changed our calculations, inspiring us to partner with another name-brand star who already had a large and loyal following.

In the mid-2000s, Criss Angel was huge. Some called him the biggest name in magic since Houdini. During a five-year run ending in 2010, his cable television hit *Criss Angel Mindfreak* made him the most-featured magician in prime-time history. Yes, Cirque would have to violate its long-standing rule against building a production around a big-name performer—"the show is the star," as we say—but his act seemed ready-made for Las Vegas. And if Cirque is about anything, it's about breaking even our own self-imposed limits and trying new things.

When *Criss Angel Believe* opened at the Luxor on October 31, 2008, the reviews were scathing—and rightly so. You know a show is in trouble when you see friends after a premiere and they want to talk about the weather, your family, mutual acquaintances—anything but the show. That night, the problem was clear: in trying to be more narrative and theatrical than usual, we ended up with the worst of both worlds. It had not nearly enough of the magic Criss Angel was known for or the awe-inspiring acts we specialize in. Trying to cram too much into one production made it fail both as a magic show and as a circus event. That was an obvious flaw that we should have caught earlier, but we were so busy cranking out three shows at once, we did not exercise enough oversight.

With ticket sales slow, we overhauled the production twice. Within a year, we decided to remove most of the Cirque acts from the stage, stay on as producer, and let Angel do his magic acts. The show recovered, running successfully until the spring of 2016, when it was replaced by *Criss Angel Mindfreak Live!*, which ran for another two years.

From a business standpoint, we looked back at those two Criss Angel shows as a success, since they ran for a total of ten years in a highly competitive Las Vegas environment. But from a creative perspective, the lesson was clear: stick with what you know; don't try to be too many things to too many people. I'm not saying that mixing artistic content can't work. We proved it can with *The Beatles LOVE*. But in that case, the crucial distinction was that the artist being celebrated was not onstage. Can you imagine doing a Beatles show with Paul McCartney sharing the stage with Cirque? It would be a disaster. Paul would say, "I don't want an acrobatic act here, I don't like this costume, and while you're at it, move those dancers over here." The Criss Angel experiment showed what happens when we sublimate our aesthetic to the needs of a star: neither of us ends up satisfied, and audience members are confused about what kind of show they're watching.

Unfortunately, the same thing happened two years later, when our Las Vegas resident show *Viva Elvis* opened at the new Aria Resort & Casino. As with Criss Angel, we turned the show over to a single personality (Elvis Presley appearing via video clips and recordings) instead of delivering a Cirque acrobatic show. We also fell into the trap that we avoided with *The Beatles LOVE*, getting seduced into telling Elvis's life story rather than creating our own visual interpretation of his music. As I am constantly reminding the directors we hire, people don't go to a Cirque performance for the story. They go to see an astonishing spectacle, which was in short supply in *Viva Elvis*. In trying to please everyone—devotees of Elvis, Cirque, and 1950s jukebox culture—we pleased no one. After less than a year and a half, the show closed in August of 2012. Note to self: no more biographical Cirque shows!

SOMETIMES YOUR BOSS CALLS
FROM OUTER SPACE

As CEO, much of the responsibility for managing the simultaneous crises of our troubled shows and the Great Recession fell on me—as well it should have. That's all part of my job. In 2009, my duties expanded further when Guy began pulling away from the company, distracted by his other passions. That was the year he reached two milestones—turning fifty years old and celebrating Cirque's twenty-fifth anniversary—and that made him hungry for new challenges. An innately restless and adventurous man, he does not like being tied down and never imagined he would remain at Cirque beyond the age of thirty. Yet here he was, twenty years later, feeling trapped.

"I was not going in a good emotional direction," Guy explained to an interviewer. "When I was on the street [performing], I could wake up and decide to go north, south, up, down, left, or right and nobody was there to tell me it wasn't possible. I needed something personal to reenergize me."

An inveterate traveler, Guy had long dreamed of making the ultimate journey, to outer space. By coincidence, during this restive period, his good friend the Canadian astronaut Julie Payette encouraged him to grab the last remaining seat as a "space tourist" on a rocket to the International Space Station. It would cost $35 million, but money was never very important to Guy—he has always been driven by a craving for new experiences. One day, he called and said, "If I want to go to outer space, it's now or never. So, I will be away from the office for the next six months to train for my great adventure!"

I couldn't believe my ears, but I was so happy for him. After eight years at Cirque, I had learned to expect a certain amount of eccentric behavior. I just never imagined that my boss would blast off into outer space! But that's all part of the package when dealing with artistic people. You must be ready for anything, including being without your company founder and creative guide for a long stretch when he decides that a ten-day trip to the International Space Station is just what he needs to recharge his batteries.

And yet Guy's motivation was not only personal. He saw this as a great opportunity to draw attention to the charitable cause he had recently founded—the One Drop Foundation, which provides clean drinking water to needy people around the world. When his six months of hard training was over, I traveled to a military base in Kazakhstan with a group of Guy's friends, family, and coworkers to witness the dramatic launch. I will never forget the sight of Guy dressed in his space suit and wearing a bulbous red nose during the solemn ceremony before liftoff, our whole entourage laughing and shaking our heads at our favorite clown. When the rocket roared into the air without incident, we all felt an enormous sense of relief.

Three days later, I was back in Montreal, driving down the highway, when my phone rang: "Hello, Daniel, it's Guy!" At that moment, I became one of the few people in human history to get a call from his boss from a space capsule orbiting Earth. He wanted to discuss details of the show he was putting on. Yes, even from way up there, Guy was still being a producer and showman. He was organizing a two-hour party, broadcast on television and streamed over the internet, to raise awareness for his One Drop Foundation. Our modern-day P. T. Barnum was producing events in fourteen cities, including Moscow, Rio de Janeiro, Montreal, and Tampa Bay, featuring music by U2 and an appearance by former US vice president Al Gore.

On October 11, 2009, Guy returned to Earth with two astronauts in the Russian Soyuz spacecraft, drifting down by parachute and landing safely on the ground in northern Kazakhstan. I was ecstatic watching news coverage of him being extracted from the capsule, again wearing his clown nose and an enormous grin. That moment was so inspirational to our employees, a powerful reminder for us all to seek out new challenges, no matter how far from our comfort zone they take us.

That doesn't mean you have to rocket to outer space like Guy or the legendary entrepreneurs Richard Branson and Jeff Bezos, who actually built their own spacecraft. Any authentic passion you pursue helps send a strong message to your colleagues about your values and those of the company.

UNDERSTAND THE LIMITS OF YOUR BRAND

While Guy was off on his adventure, our troubles intensified. The global economy was still struggling, but we had yet to learn our lesson about slowing down. Clearly, we should have either stopped producing new shows entirely for a while or limited ourselves to just one. Instead, we brazenly forged ahead with two more in 2009—*Ovo* in April and *Banana Shpeel* in November.

Had we focused only on *Ovo*, a show inspired by the insect world that fell squarely within the Cirque tradition, we might have been fine. Our world-class artists, costumed beautifully as ladybugs, dragonflies, spiders, butterflies, and cockroaches, wowed the audience with daring trampoline, aerial silk, hoop, and trapeze acts. Despite the downturn, *Ovo* sold tickets briskly and toured for more than a decade.

Banana Shpeel was an entirely different story. It was, without a doubt, the biggest flop in Cirque's history. Our production was based on an exciting idea: since we had reinvented the circus arts, maybe we could do the same with other stale performance genres, starting with vaudeville. Born in France in the nineteenth century, vaudeville's circus-like blend of music, comedy, magic, ventriloquism, clowns, jugglers, and more made it hugely popular in the United States and Canada until the early 1930s. If Cirque could revive vaudeville with a modern spin, we might create a whole new category of live entertainment, establishing another market with few competitors, just as we did with the circus.

Our plan was to open in Chicago in late 2009 for an out-of-town tryout. Once the kinks were worked out, we would conquer New York with a permanent residency at the magnificently restored 2,900-seat Beacon Theatre in Manhattan. Since our mantra is to constantly challenge ourselves—and we would be competing with story-heavy Broadway shows—we decided to depart from our usual emphasis on acrobatics in favor of a more narrative style. We were excited to sign up as writer and director David Shiner, already a Cirque legend for his stellar clown performance in our early touring show *Nouvelle Expérience*. David went on to cocreate the Tony Award–winning Broadway show *Fool Moon* in 1993 and wrote and directed our touring production *Kooza*, which premiered in 2007.

David and his team created a narrative, interspersed with music and dancing, about a loud, ambitious theatrical producer named Marty Schmelky, who interacts with idiotic sidekicks; his beleaguered assistant Margaret; and a trio of clowns who crash his auditions and create havoc. There were some acrobatic acts, but none of the truly astonishing trapeze, strap, and other airborne stunts our fans had come to expect.

Even during the development process, a festering problem was evident: the project was usually discussed in terms of what we *didn't* want instead of what we *did* want. We conspicuously avoided labels that we thought would limit us, like *Broadway* or *musical theater*. As a result, there was never a clear vision of what the show would *be*.

When *Banana Shpeel* opened in Chicago in November of 2009, the critics were merciless. The *Daily Herald* called it "an incomprehensible mess," and the *Windy City Times* wondered, "How could a show with such vast resources turn out to be so mired in puerility and tedium?" Ouch! Some audience members who had never seen a Cirque show before seemed to enjoy it, but our loyal fans left the theater extremely disappointed.

Still, we thought we could save the show. When the Chicago run ended, we moved into the Beacon Theatre and overhauled the production, delaying its opening from early February to late April of 2010. Knowing the high standards of the sophisticated audience and critics in New York, we increased our $20 million budget by another $5 million, changed the story line, added new acts, and replaced some actors. But that only made it worse. We did not have the option of transforming the show into a more typical high-flying Cirque production because the Beacon Theatre was an old landmark building that could not support the elaborate rigging we require—and we certainly couldn't tear up the place, as we routinely do in the modern Las Vegas resorts.

When Guy came to a dress rehearsal before previews, he probably wished he had stayed in outer space. After watching the show—an uninspiring mash-up of vaudeville, theater, clowning, and acrobatics—he sat on the floor of the lobby with Gilles Ste-Croix and me, shook his head, and said, "My God, what is this? It's so *bad*." It was too late to cancel opening night, so we took a deep breath and launched the show anyway. Once again, reviews were negative and ticket sales were weak. During the run, we did a market study and the results came back: if we kept going, our brand would suffer greatly.

In late June of 2010, after less than two months, we shut the show down. We made a last-ditch effort to revive it, opening in

Toronto in September. But after three weeks, we closed *Banana Shpeel* down again for the last time. All in all, we lost about $8 million. Our partner, the Madison Square Garden Corporation, owner of the Beacon Theatre, also lost $8 million on the show. But the president of MSG's entertainment division at the time, Jay Marciano, was incredibly understanding and supportive during the entire ordeal. As a veteran of the live-entertainment industry, he knew all too well that shows can be hit or miss. His patience and goodwill resulted in a strong ongoing relationship between Cirque and AEG, our partner in some touring productions around the world, where Jay is now chief operating officer.

There are many lessons to draw from the *Banana Shpeel* episode. Clearly, we should have caught problems much earlier in the show's development. We should have defined our mission more clearly. For me, our biggest failure was not being aware of the limits of our brand. Yes, we always want to break ground with a new show, but we must do it a way that makes it recognizably Cirque du Soleil. Instead, we committed the same mistake we made with *Criss Angel Believe* and *Viva Elvis*: it just didn't feel like a Cirque show. If we had made a conscious decision from the start to depart radically from our past and focus strictly on a modern vaudeville show, without any acrobatics at all, the gamble might have paid off—but only if we removed the Cirque du Soleil name from our advertising so people would not be under any false illusions about what to expect.

When you ask someone leaving a Cirque du Soleil show to describe what they just saw, they often say it's not really a circus, not a musical, not an opera, and not a dance show. "It's really all those things," they say. That's a good explanation of how we created a new category of live entertainment. Our fans arrive at our big-top tents, theaters, and arenas expecting to have a unique experience with stunning visuals and breathtaking acrobatics. If we don't give it to them, they leave disappointed, and our brand suffers.

This lesson can be applied to any industry. If you are running a French restaurant, your customers will be very confused if you start serving burritos and tacos. A wellness company should stay away from controversial remedies that may be bad for your health. No matter how profitable such deviations may seem, it's usually best to avoid the risk of harming the company's image. If your customers are unhappy with the changes, cut your losses as soon as possible. Yes, we lost a lot of money on *Banana Shpeel* when we shut it down, but stubbornly continuing could have done extensive damage to our brand. That's not a risk worth taking.

PROVIDE A SAFE ENVIRONMENT

Lest you think Cirque had completely gone off the rails, I should point out that we also had a number of great successes during this period. Our touring production *Totem* (2010), directed by *KÀ* creator Robert LePage, drew heavily on mythology to brilliantly celebrate the evolution of humanity. We tapped François Girard, director of the acclaimed *Thirty Two Short Films About Glenn Gould*, to create *Zarkana* (2011) about a magician who meets a series of fantastical creatures during a surreal adventure. *Zarkana* sold out Radio City Music Hall in New York and Moscow's Kremlin Palace before moving to Madrid and then replacing *Viva Elvis* at the Aria Resort in Las Vegas. For *Iris*, a resident show at the Kodak Theatre in Los Angeles (2011), former *Zumanity* director Philippe Decouflé created a stunning experience using images from the history of cinema (though LA proved to be a difficult market for live entertainment, and *Iris* closed after sixteen months). *Amaluna* (2012), created by theater and opera director Diane Paulus, was a dazzling woman-centric production inspired by Shakespeare's *The Tempest* that proved to be enormously popular.

In the midst of our comeback, disaster struck again—but this time it was not our doing. On March 11, 2011, the most powerful earthquake ever recorded in Japan triggered a monstrous tsunami that washed ashore with thirty-foot waves, killing more than ten thousand people and causing a meltdown at the Fukushima Daiichi Nuclear Power Plant. With two shows running in Tokyo at the time—*Zed* at Tokyo Disney and our touring show *Kooza*—we immediately went into full crisis mode.

The tsunami hit on a Friday, so I spent a chaotic weekend trying to ensure the safety of our three hundred employees. While most of the flooding happened far from Tokyo, lethal radioactivity was still spewing from the crippled Fukushima reactor and authorities feared it would reach the city. As I furiously worked the phones, I was caught in a tug-of-war. Our partners in Japan begged me to keep our staff in place so we could quickly resume the shows once things returned to normal. Employees and their families, on the other hand, were desperate to leave the country as soon as possible.

I knew all our employees were watching me closely and would judge us based upon what we decided. I had repeatedly told them, in my annual presentations, that we would always keep them safe. Now was the time to make good on that promise. Airlifting our entire team out of Japan would mean a major financial loss, but there is no use looking at the numbers at moments like this. We resolved to get our employees out as quickly as possible, buying three hundred plane tickets and relocating the entire cast and crew of both shows to Macao. There they could continue training at the facilities of our resident show *Zaia* until the situation in Japan improved.

Based on my experience with managing crises earlier in my career, I knew it was important to act quickly and decisively. Our partners ended up agreeing with our decision to get our employees out when it became clear that the threat of radioactive fallout was not diminishing. As it turns out, the toxic cloud did not reach Tokyo, but we had no way of knowing that at the time. Had the city become radioactive, I never would have forgiven myself for leaving my team behind. Our employees would not have forgiven us either. Instead, our people were impressed by how rapidly and thoroughly we took care of them.

After a short hiatus—four weeks for *Kooza*, six weeks for *Zed*—the shows reopened in April. The Japanese economy was so devastated that we had to close *Zed* for good by the end of the year. But in every other way, the production was a triumph, running for more than a thousand performances and selling one million tickets faster than any previous show in Japan's history.

Providing a safe environment for employees is one of the most important responsibilities of every company leader—especially in creative organizations because there is so much risk involved. Sometimes that risk is emotional and psychological as we open ourselves up and become more vulnerable, making it crucial that we offer a safe space free from hasty judgment or unconstructive criticism. Sometimes the risk is physical, as with the incredibly daring feats our artists perform that seem to defy the normal limits of human potential.

At Cirque, we have always taken very seriously the need to protect our people from the dangers inherent in circus acts— especially as the industry's stage technology becomes more

(Above left) Madame Zazou, Cirque du Soleil's internal clown, gearing me up for the relaunch of our shows. MARC-ANTOINE CHARLEBOIS—2021. *(Above right) During his visit to Montreal in 2017, I met President Barack Obama to discuss potential collaborations between Cirque du Soleil and the Obama Foundation.* PERSONAL COLLECTION

(Above left) With my dear friend and founder of Cirque du Soleil, Guy Laliberté, on the Hollywood Walk of Fame, when he received his star in 2010. PERSONAL COLLECTION. *(Above right) With the two cochairmen of Cirque du Soleil, Jim Murren and Gabriel de Alba, and our new CEO, Stéphane Lefebvre.* ©CIRQUE DU SOLEIL 2021

A view of the Cirque du Soleil iconic big top in the Old Port of Montreal. PRODUCTIONS ACEMEDIA

Corteo Hula Hoop Act. Costumes by Dominique Lemieux. ©CIRQUE DU SOLEIL 2018

Musicians perform in the Tempête Act of Crystal. ©CIRQUE DU SOLEIL PHOTO MATT BEARD—2020

Acrobatics and skating collide in the Tempête Act of Crystal. ©CIRQUE DU SOLEIL PHOTO MATT BEARD—2020

Jugglers display an incredible set of skills while on skates during the Juggling Act of Crystal. ©CIRQUE DU
SOLEIL PHOTO MATT BEARD—2020

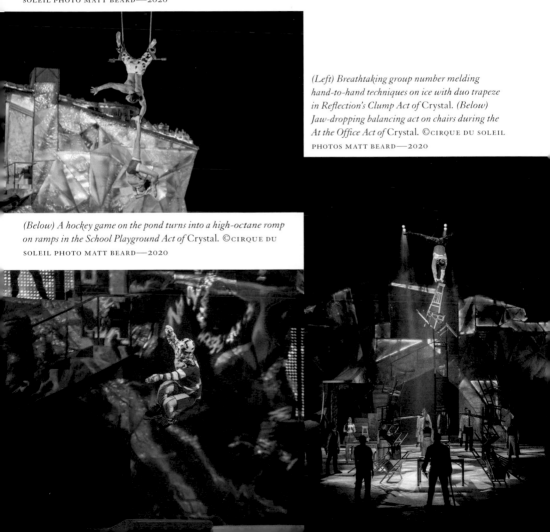

*(Left) Breathtaking group number melding
hand-to-hand techniques on ice with duo trapeze
in Reflection's Clump Act of* Crystal. *(Below)
Jaw-dropping balancing act on chairs during the
At the Office Act of* Crystal. ©CIRQUE DU SOLEIL
PHOTOS MATT BEARD—2020

*(Below) A hockey game on the pond turns into a high-octane romp
on ramps in the School Playground Act of* Crystal. ©CIRQUE DU
SOLEIL PHOTO MATT BEARD—2020

The Skeleton Dance in Kooza. ©CIRQUE DU SOLEIL COSTUMES MARIE-CHANTALE VAILLANCOURT; PHOTO MATT BEARD—2020

(Above) The Trickster from Kooza. *(Right) The Charivari Act, combining acrobatics, rapid-fire costume changes, and rebounds from three miniature trampolines set on the stage, in* Kooza. ©CIRQUE DU SOLEIL COSTUMES MARIE-CHANTALE VAILLANCOURT; PHOTOS MATT BEARD—2018

The indispensable sidekicks in the extravagant adventures in the realm of Kooza. ©CIRQUE DU SOLEIL COSTUMES MARIE-CHANTALE VAILLANCOURT; PHOTO MATT BEARD—2018

Young performers work in harmony and unison during the Contortion Act of Kooza. ©CIRQUE DU SOLEIL COSTUMES MARIE-CHANTALE VAILLANCOURT; PHOTO MATT BEARD—2018

(Above) The Grand Finale of Kooza. (Right) The Hoops Manipulation Act, combining fluidity of movement, physical contortion, exceptional balance, and impressive dexterity, from Kooza. ©CIRQUE DU SOLEIL COSTUMES MARIE-CHANTALE VAILLANCOURT; PHOTOS MATT BEARD—2018

A trapeze artist performs a series of original figures in the Roue Cyr Act of LUZIA. ©CIRQUE DU SOLEIL PHOTO MATT BEARD—2019

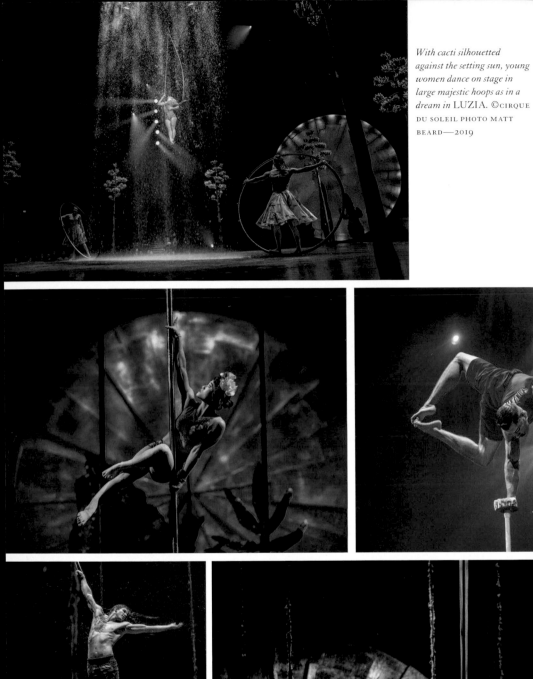

With cacti silhouetted against the setting sun, young women dance on stage in large majestic hoops as in a dream in LUZIA. ©CIRQUE DU SOLEIL PHOTO MATT BEARD—2019

(Above, left to right) A puppeteer from LUZIA *wearing the* charro *shirt, the traditional men's suit in Mexico; a female character is wrapped in an iguana shawl, an ode to the Mexican surrealist movement, in* LUZIA; *fish heads from* LUZIA. ©CIRQUE DU SOLEIL PHOTOS MATT BEARD—2019

(Left) In a dreamlike setting, acrobats climb up and down vertical poles during the Masts and Poles Act of LUZIA; *a lifeguard struts about on a buoy among the waves in a tribute to Mexican cinema of the 1920s in the Canes Act of* LUZIA. ©CIRQUE DU SOLEIL PHOTOS MATT BEARD—2019

(Below, left to right) The artist's hair whips the surface of the water as he rotates on the straps in a circle just above the water during the Aerial Straps Act in LUZIA; *the graceful Aerial Straps Act above water from* LUZIA; *an artist representing a demigod of rain emerging from the pristine waters of a* cenote *during the Aerial Straps Act in* LUZIA. ©CIRQUE DU SOLEIL PHOTOS MATT BEARD—2019

(Right) Youthful performance paying tribute to the modern ritual sport of football, which is highly celebrated in Mexico, in the Football Dance Act of LUZIA. *(Far right) Acrobats climbing up and down vertical poles and crisscrossing in the air from* LUZIA. ©CIRQUE DU SOLEIL PHOTOS MATT BEARD—2019

An artist displaying his great physical strength during the Hand Balancing Act in LUZIA. ©CIRQUE DU SOLEIL PHOTO MATT BEARD—2019

Aerial Straps Act above the surface of the water in LUZIA. ©CIRQUE DU SOLEIL PHOTO MATT BEARD—2019

The Hoop Diving Act in LUZIA *is a roaring tribute to agility and speed.* ©CIRQUE DU SOLEIL PHOTO MATT BEARD—2019

As the morning sun rises, a woman and a metallic horse run together to awaken an imaginary Mexico in the Running Woman Act of LUZIA. ©CIRQUE DU SOLEIL PHOTO MATT BEARD—2019

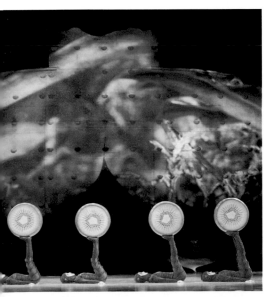

(Above left) Astonishing display of precision juggling from the Foot Juggling Act of Ovo. *(Above right) A pair of butterflies performs a pas-de-deux on aerial straps in* Ovo. ©CIRQUE DU SOLEIL PHOTOS VLADIMIR LORENZO—2017

(Above, left) A Spider defies gravity and physics in a succession of seemingly impossible feats of strength and balance in the Slackwire Act of Ovo. ©CIRQUE DU SOLEIL PHOTO CLAUDE DUFRESNE, SNAPEPHOTO—2017; *(Above, right) The Diabolos Act of Ovo is a mix of high-speed diabolo and seemingly impossible juggling.* ©CIRQUE DU SOLEIL PHOTO VLADIMIR LORENZO—2017

(Left) Group shot of Ovo artists on stage. (Below) the iconic egg of Ovo. ©CIRQUE DU SOLEIL PHOTOS VLADIMIR LORENZO—2017. *(Below left) The Foreigner and The Ladybug perform in Ovo.* ©CIRQUE DU SOLEIL PHOTO PATRICK BEAUDRY, SNAPEPHOTO—2017

(Above) A Dragonfly performs a graceful balancing act in the Orvalho act of Ovo. ©CIRQUE DU SOLEIL
PHOTO VLADIMIR LORENZO—2017

Aerial Strap Act from Ovo *merging hand-to-hand, ballet, and aerial contortion.* ©CIRQUE DU SOLEIL PHOTO VLADIMIR LORENZO—2017

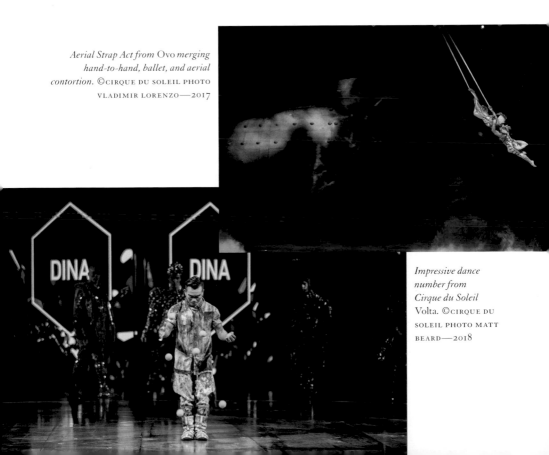

Impressive dance number from Cirque du Soleil Volta. ©CIRQUE DU SOLEIL PHOTO MATT BEARD—2018

(Left) Rope skipping takes on a new dimension with a heightened level of acrobatic prowess in the Mr. Wow Show Rope Skipping Act of Volta. (Below) A spellbinding artist, suspended only by her hair, levitating slowly above the stage in the Mirage Act of Volta. ©CIRQUE DU SOLEIL PHOTOS MATT BEARD—2018

Volta artist flying majestically in long sweeping arcs during the Acro Lamp Act. ©CIRQUE DU SOLEIL PHOTO MATT BEARD—2018

Riders invade the stage to deliver a jaw-dropping, fast, and furious performance of nonstop acrobatics on wheels for the finale of Volta. ©CIRQUE DU SOLEIL PHOTO MATT BEARD—2018

(Far left) Two FREESPIRITS *perform a daring hand-to-hand duo while rolling on a unicycle in the Precision Walk/ Unicycle Act from* Volta. *(Left) Artists climb, spin, and execute acrobatic and artistic figures on the ladders in synchronized and alternating patterns during the Leaving the City Act of* Volta. ©CIRQUE DU SOLEIL PHOTOS MATT BEARD—2018

(Below, left) Guy Laliberté and I hosting actor Michael Douglas, a big fan of Cirque du Soleil. (Below, right) Enjoying the premiere of the Blue Man Group Speechless Tour in Montreal, Canada. PERSONAL COLLECTION

Our former chief of creation Jean-François Bouchard and I bringing Elon Musk behind the scenes of Kurios: Cabinet of Curiosities *in Los Angeles.* PERSONAL COLLECTION

(Below, left) Standing in Cirque du Soleil's creative headquarters in Montreal, Canada, 2016. (Below, right) Sir Paul McCartney at The Beatles LOVE *premiere, Las Vegas, June 2006.* PERSONAL COLLECTION

(Below, left) The King of Pop, Michael Jackson, visiting our Montreal headquarters in 2001 with Lyn Heward, former president Cirque's Creative Content Division. (Below, right) Fun time with the Jackson Brothers at the Michael Jackson ONE *premiere in Vegas.* PERSONAL COLLECTION

James Cameron and his partner Jon Landau at the premiere of our Avatar *live show in December 2015.*
©CIRQUE DU SOLEIL—2015

My friend James Cameron, whom I had the pleasure to work with on Toruk: The First Flight. PERSONAL COLLECTION

Daniel Chávez, owner of the Vidanta Group, and I at the press conference announcing the new dinner show project between Cirque du Soleil and Grupo Vidanta, May 2014.
PERSONAL COLLECTION

Alegria *by Cirque du Soleil.* ©cirque du soleil—1994; Mystère *by Cirque du Soleil.* ©cirque du soleil—1993; Alegria: In a New Light *by Cirque du Soleil.* ©cirque du soleil—2019; Toruk: The First Flight *by Cirque du Soleil.* ©cirque du soleil—2015

Saltimbanco *by Cirque du Soleil.* ©cirque du soleil—1992; Michael Jackson ONE *by Cirque du Soleil.* ©cirque du soleil—2013; The Beatles LOVE *by Cirque du Soleil.* ©cirque du soleil—2006; O *by Cirque du Soleil.* ©cirque du soleil—1998

Nouvelle Expérience *by Cirque du Soleil.* ©cirque du soleil—1990; Varekai *by Cirque du Soleil.* ©cirque du soleil—2006

complex. For the water show *O*, for example, we developed an intricate system of safety checks using scuba divers who serve as underwater stagehands, electricians, and carpenters to make sure everything is functioning properly. Performers receive extensive safety training that includes perfecting maneuvers on the ground before attempting them in the air. Our artists are in constant radio contact with safety personnel, and we have multiple rescue plans for every act in every show. Our safety measures are so stringent, in fact, that our artists often find them confining and annoying. Many prefer to rely on their own skill and bravery. Still, we insist.

Our safety record is phenomenal considering the thousands of shows we put on, all around the world, during a normal year. Unfortunately, as with every industry, accidents do happen. For nearly thirty years, we never had a show fatality. Then, one night in June of 2013, just as we seemed to be emerging from the most challenging period in Cirque's history, our worst nightmare came true.

I remember the night well. With wine and good spirits flowing, I was enjoying myself at the gala reception following the premiere of our new Las Vegas show, *Michael Jackson ONE*. One of our employees interrupted my conversation with Jim Murren, the chief executive of MGM Resorts International, requesting to talk to me. A bit annoyed, I politely said I was in the middle of a conversation, but he insisted, pulling me away to whisper that there had been a terrible accident during our showing of *KÀ*. One of our artists was hovering between life and death. Shocked, I offered a quick apology and left the party to head to my hotel room, where we set up a crisis-response unit. I was informed that the artist was Sarah Guyard-Guillot, a thirty-one-year-old acrobat from Paris who fell when a safety wire had accidentally become detached. An hour later, we were horrified to learn that she died from her injuries.

Emotions run strong at such moments, but there was no time to lapse into despair. I had to stay focused on the important work at hand: attend to Sarah's ex-husband, who also worked on *KÀ*, and their two children. We had to cooperate with the coroner and government officials, who immediately began an investigation. We also had to communicate with both the media and our devastated employees.

The next morning, I met with the Las Vegas cast and crew of *KÀ*, one of the most painful events of my life. Tears were shed, including my own. I knew that my main job was to make them all feel safe and secure. So, after acknowledging the shock and grief we all felt, I said they would not have to return to the stage until they felt completely ready: "It will be up to you to decide when the show goes back on." I assured them that Sarah's children would be taken care of. In addition to what our life insurance plan provided, we later set up a trust fund for college expenses for the two children when they grew up. We also bought plane tickets for Sarah's family members in Europe so they could attend the funeral. Our human resources department set up an employee support team staffed by expert psychologists who specialize in such crises. In these and other ways, we went beyond the usual corporate obligations because we think of our employees as family. It was important to demonstrate kindness, compassion, and generosity. To help all of us grieve, we organized a private funeral service for family and friends.

After a two-week hiatus, the artists told us they were ready to start training again. The show resumed a few days later.

I wish I could say that was the only time we endured such an ordeal, but three years later, our forty-three-year-old technician,

Olivier Rochette, died after being struck by a telescopic lift while setting up for our touring show *Luzia* in San Francisco. This was especially traumatic because Olivier was the son of our cofounder Gilles Ste-Croix. I had to call Gilles myself to deliver the news, another wrenching moment that haunts me still. And our aerial straps performer Yann Arnaud, thirty-eight, died in 2018 after falling during a performance of *Volta* in Tampa.

Each time, I went to the site of the show and met with the cast and crew. As with the first incident, I left it up to them to decide when to reopen the show. It was crucial, I felt, that employees did not feel they were under any pressure from the company. Our economic losses did not matter; our paramount concern was their health and well-being.

It's certainly true that, as the volume of our shows increased, the potential for accidents rose somewhat. But even after such terrible incidents, our employees know that every precaution has been taken. No shows can open without a thorough analysis of safety measures by official bodies such as the US government's Occupational Safety and Health Administration (OSHA), not to mention our own stringent procedures, which go well beyond what the law requires.

Another commitment we take very seriously is to protect the job of every employee—but here again, there are moments when that is impossible. No company is immune from large market forces that can knock it off-balance, and we were certainly no exception. Though Cirque steadfastly resisted widespread lay-offs during the worst years of the global recession, by the end of 2012 revenues had declined too sharply to prevent it. Because our shows have such a long development period, the impact of the downturn was somewhat delayed. But it certainly caught up with us. In the span of just over a year, four of our productions closed, starting with *Zed* in late December 2011, continuing with *Zaia* and *Viva Elvis* the following year, and then *Iris* in January 2013.

With so many shows closing at the same time, we didn't have enough new productions coming up to rehire our dedicated casts and crews. By then, we had finally begun to restrain ourselves, cutting back to one new show per year. So, on January 16, 2013, we announced the agonizing decision to lay off four hundred people, about 8 percent of our five thousand employees.

It was a distressing experience for everyone and certainly one of the worst days of my life. I remained upbeat in public, but in private I was despondent. When I spoke with my peers at other big entertainment companies, they did not understand why I was so upset. For them, cost cutting through layoffs was just business as usual. For us, it was high drama. Cirque had always been so profitable that we never had to go through something like this before. Fortunately, most of our employees knew that we would not have resorted to such an extreme measure unless we truly had no other choice. They understood that the future of the company was at stake.

When that storm subsided, things began looking up for Cirque. Our rate of producing new shows had slowed to a more sustainable pace, and 2013 looked very promising. A successful touring show we had developed during this period, 2011's *Michael Jackson: The Immortal World Tour,* was being revamped into a spectacular resident show opening in May at the Mandalay Bay Resort and Casino in Las Vegas.

Like a clown who had slipped on a banana peel, Cirque was rising up, dusting itself off, and getting back to work.

CHAPTER 5

MASTERING NEW CREATIVE CHALLENGES

Cirque du Soleil's comeback began with a tragedy.

On June 25, 2009, Michael Jackson died from cardiac arrest after overdosing on sleep medications. He was such a revered artist that it was only a matter of time before somebody staged a tribute concert for his millions of mourning fans worldwide (which included many of us at Cirque). The most likely candidate was the Anschutz Entertainment Group (AEG), the giant sports-and-music firm that was preparing to produce his run of fifty sold-out shows at London's O2 Arena, scheduled to start less than three weeks before he died. The event would have broken records for the biggest concert-series audience ever to see an artist in a single city.

Michael was a huge Cirque fan, having attended nearly all our shows. He even asked for a private tour of our Montreal headquarters soon after I started working there. I will never forget the day I spent showing him around with his two young children. Michael was mesmerized by our costume department and spent nearly the entire visit there, asking to see one dazzling ensemble and goofy clown outfit after another. Before he left, he suggested that maybe we could work together someday. When he died, I regretted the missed opportunity and began imagining how we might stage an event celebrating his life. Then I let the idea go. Given the mega concert series it had been planning, AEG was such an obvious choice to produce a Michael Jackson tribute that it seemed foolish to waste my time even thinking about it.

LISTEN TO YOUR EMPLOYEES

But somehow, I couldn't forget the idea—and neither could our employees. As I passed people in the corridor, they would say, "Daniel, when are we doing a Michael Jackson show?" By then, *The Beatles LOVE* had been playing to sold-out houses in Vegas for three years, so everyone knew we had the skills to create a fabulous event around an iconic performer. And yet I was sure that AEG had the inside track.

This back-and-forth continued for days: employees would ask me about it, and I would shrug. I'm sure I was being much too timid, probably leery of being rejected. Our people knew better, practically shaking me by the lapels and shouting, "Daniel, wake up! We *have* to do a Michael Jackson show!"

Finally, I gathered up the courage to call Michael's estate and reached John Branca. Many years earlier, John had replaced the star's father, Joseph Jackson, as his manager and had become coexecutor of his estate. "Funny you should call—we were just talking about you," he said. "Michael's mom called yesterday and said if there is one company in the world that would be perfect to do a tribute show, it would be Cirque du Soleil."

I hung up the phone grinning from ear to ear. Now, as I walked down the corridor, I would say, "Guess who I just called? We're doing a Michael Jackson show!"

Looking back, the lesson is clear: to be a truly creative company, you must listen carefully to your employees. After all, you have hired them to be proactive and think big, so why ignore their ideas? Sometimes they can see things more clearly than decision-makers, who can only imagine the many roadblocks and endless practical reasons why some bold new project can't work.

Listening to your employees can save you from disaster. I've noticed many examples of that in the business world. Take Samsung. Some of its employees warned that the design of its Galaxy Note 7 was very risky. The company ignored their pleas and released the smartphone anyway in August of 2016. Within weeks, the devices started exploding and catching fire, causing Samsung to recall and finally discontinue the line. All it took to prevent billions in losses and serious damage to the company's brand was to pay attention to the workers who knew the product best.

DO YOUR RESEARCH

As excited as I was about how warmly we were received by Michael Jackson's estate, I knew I still had a long way to go to complete a deal. Other well-known producers were making their pitches, and I knew I would have to use every tool in my kit to pull this off.

By then, I had come to see business negotiations as a creative process, one that requires a good bit of imagination and spontaneity. Research is a key element, telling you not only who the main players are but what buttons to press when you speak to them. The other coexecutor of the estate was Michael's longtime friend John McClain. I knew we had no chance of landing this deal unless I could persuade both Branca and McClain that Cirque was the only partner they would ever need.

When we met in Los Angeles, I could see that Branca was mostly on my side, but McClain was not convinced. I had to think fast. Then I remembered that McClain was a die-hard fan of the Los Angeles Lakers. I knew that the Lakers, led by Kobe Bryant, had recently become NBA champions, defeating the Orlando Magic in five games. So I turned to McClain and said, "Listen, all of this basically comes down to making a choice: Would you rather play for the Lakers or the Orlando Magic?"

I knew it was risky to compare ourselves to that legendary basketball franchise. But just as Guy saw no problem putting Cirque on the same creative level as the Beatles, I was convinced that we could live up to the artistry of Michael Jackson. The gambit worked. McClain began to see us as the LA Lakers of the entertainment world, and soon we struck an agreement. Ever since then, whenever we meet, McClain still calls me the Lakers guy—a reminder to do my research next time I engage in a difficult negotiation.

BEWARE OF COMPLACENCY

As with the Beatles, we did not want to merely license the rights to Michael Jackson's music. Any producer can do that—but licensing music doesn't give you the right to use the images of the artist, whether you're a tribute band like Beatlemania or an Elvis impersonator. Obviously, we had no interest in that kind of copycat approach. Our goal is always to get permission from the actual performers or their estates and to work closely with them to create a fresh interpretation of their work.

Our plan was to first launch a touring show, *Michael Jackson: The Immortal World Tour*, which premiered in October of 2011 (starting off in Montreal, as usual). We already had *Zarkana* and

Iris in the pipeline to open that same year, so it made me a bit nervous to take on another ambitious project at a time when we were trying to slow down our pace of production in the wake of the global financial crisis. But it's not every day that you get to celebrate a legend like Michael Jackson, so I felt we had to push ahead, despite the risks.

If we planned well enough, we thought we could simultaneously create a separate show at the Mandalay Bay Resort in Las Vegas that we would call *Michael Jackson ONE*. Because resident productions are far more complex and require the full renovation of a theater, that show would take much longer and could not open until two years later. Both would be directed by Jamie King, a dancer who toured with Michael and later directed concert tours of stars like Madonna, Celine Dion, and Britney Spears. As with the Beatles show, we reimagined and remixed Michael's original recordings, this time using Rihanna producer Kevin Antunes, to create a beautiful musical landscape that would drive the show. We also assembled a team of top choreographers, some of whom had worked with Michael himself.

A touring show is quite a different beast than a resident production, of course. On tour, we have to travel as lightly as possible, which limits our technical possibilities. Our Las Vegas water show, *O*, for example, could never tour because it would be impossible to travel with a 1.5-million-gallon pool. *Michael Jackson: The Immortal World Tour* was like an arena rock concert, primarily a musical production with dancing and some acrobatics. Resident productions, on the other hand, allow for much more elaborate rigging and design. So Jamie came up with an entirely new concept for the Las Vegas show, creating a story of four "misfits"—Clumsy, Shy, Smarty Pants, and Sneaky—who journey into Michael Jackson's world and emerge changed and uplifted by the experience.

The touring show was an enormous success, selling over $100 million in tickets in North America in its first two months, becoming the continent's top touring act. From there, the production moved to twenty-seven countries in Europe, Asia, Australia, New Zealand, and the Middle East, ending back in North America in August of 2014, having racked up $371 million in revenue. That placed it, at the time, as the eighth highest-grossing tour ever, according to *Billboard* magazine.

But success can easily lead to complacency. The triumph of one product does not mean your next one will also be a hit, even if they are similar. Look no further than Coca-Cola's disastrous introduction of New Coke in the mid-1980s that was "a blunder and a disaster," in the words of then CEO Roberto Goizueta. Customers can be finicky about a beloved product, so you must be extremely careful before tinkering with it.

In our case, the raves about the Michael Jackson touring show helped cause hubris to set in. We were sure we had another winner. But despite the big head start we had in exploring Michael's body of work while creating *The Immortal World Tour* and our all-star team of directors, choreographers, and performing artists, *Michael Jackson ONE* was clearly in trouble just one month before opening.

We knew something was wrong when we invited our partners from the Michael Jackson estate to their first rehearsal in Las Vegas. It was awful, and everybody knew it. Our partners were upset and demanded that we immediately postpone the premiere. After more than a decade at Cirque, however, I knew even our most successful shows can take a long time to come together and that it was important not to panic. "Give us one week," I implored them. "And if we can't fix the show, we will postpone opening night."

They agreed, and Guy jumped in to work his magic. Being very specific in his directions, he removed one act entirely and reorganized the sequence of the others. This required a great deal of work from our production teams, but they were used to it. Putting a show together is such an intricate and delicate process that there is often no way of knowing how well it's working until you are perilously close to opening night. That requires a cast and crew who are experienced, agile, and nimble enough to overhaul a show at a moment's notice.

When Michael Jackson's people returned a week later, they were flabbergasted. It was like watching a completely different show, they said—one they enjoyed immensely. "How did you do that?!" they cried. I just smiled, shrugged, and replied, "That's what we do."

Michael Jackson ONE was an immediate sensation when it premiered in Vegas in June of 2013, and it went on to become our second-best-selling show, after *O*. Especially after the failure of *Viva Elvis*, it was important for us to prove that *The Beatles LOVE* was not a fluke. *MJ ONE* proved that we had, indeed, invented a new category of show—productions based on the work of a famous artist that could appeal to fans of both the artist and of Cirque. (Out of respect, we temporarily withdrew our advertising in 2019 after HBO aired the documentary *Leaving Neverland*, in which two men alleged sexual abuse by the star. I won't attempt to litigate the facts and issues raised by the film except to say that, despite some complaints, the market decided the show should go on. Ticket sales dipped briefly, then recovered strongly as Michael's legion of fans remained steadfast in their support.)

In terms of revenue generated, *Michael Jackson ONE* today ranks fifth in the history of popular-music shows (after two each by the Rolling Stones and U2). Just as importantly, it boosted our company morale after a difficult few years. The high spirits at company headquarters returned as we got back to what we do best—producing cutting-edge, sold-out shows that receive great reviews. We vowed to be on guard against complacency, knowing that we can't always rely on Guy and our amazing production teams to dig us out of a hole at the eleventh hour. But we had pulled a rabbit out of the hat yet again—a promising sign that our comeback had begun.

DEVELOP TALENT FROM WITHIN

In chapter 2, I talked about the importance of bringing in outside talent to stimulate new thinking within your organization. Hiring Robert LePage (*KÀ*, *Totem*) and Dominic Champagne (*Varekai*, *Zumanity*, *LOVE*) was a big turning point for us: we proved that Cirque did not have to be reliant on the vision of a single staff director, no matter how brilliant that director may be.

But circumstances change, and if creativity means anything, it means being able to adapt. After more than a decade of success with a series of extraordinary outside directors, we realized that we might have drifted too far in the other direction. We were ignoring a crucial process that every company must master to stay competitive: developing talent from within.

This is not as simple as it sounds. For one thing, managers can fall into the trap of taking their own employees for granted. You see them perform their jobs every day without realizing that they may have hidden talents or the capacity for greater responsibility. It's easy to put people into a box, making it impossible for them to stretch out. Industries like law and financial services are notorious for this tendency, making employees wait for decades before being promoted to positions of real authority. Younger, more nimble companies, especially in the tech sector, often do a better job of encouraging mobility within the firm. The passion and ingenuity of employees are some of the most valuable resources a company has. If they have the skills—or at least the potential—and understand your culture and values better than any outsider would, why not give them a chance?

At Cirque, it took us a while to realize that we had a sparkling gem, hiding in plain sight, named Michel Laprise. After spending nearly a decade as an actor and theater director, he came to work in our casting department in 2000. During his first few years, Cirque was achieving great success with outside directors, so there was no established path for someone like Michel to move up to the director's chair. We didn't even know he had wanted to direct a Cirque show since his boyhood in Quebec City, when he pulled up a canvas tent flap and was astonished to catch his first glimpse of a Cirque show.

After a few years in the casting department, Michel gathered up the courage to ask Guy about directing. They both knew he wasn't ready yet to take charge of a $30 million touring show, but Michel clearly had lots of potential. So we started him out with a series of smaller assignments, which we call "special events," that celebrated important moments: the launch of the Fiat Bravo in Italy (2007); Quebec City's four hundredth anniversary (2008), Microsoft products at the 2010 Electronic Entertainment Expo, and the 2012 Super Bowl with a halftime show featuring Madonna (whose world tour he would later direct).

As Michel developed into a first-rate director, Guy knew he was ready to take on a touring show, which became 2014's

Kurios: Cabinet of Curiosities. It was the first time since Franco Dragone left fourteen years earlier that we had hired one of our own to direct. The mandate was simple: "Get back to basics." After a string of productions built around famous artists (the Beatles, Elvis, Michael Jackson) or nonacrobatic themes (*Criss Angel Believe, Banana Shpeel*), we wanted to get back to a classic Cirque show and wow crowds with what we do best: spectacular acrobatics. Michel seemed like the perfect choice, a casting expert who not only deeply understood our company and its culture but also had the imagination and drive to make the show feel fresh and new.

Michel and his team settled on a steampunk theme revolving around a late-nineteenth-century genius who tries to reinvent the world with strange contraptions and encounters fantastical creatures that are half-human, half-machine. Going from special events to a full show was a big leap for Michel, and there were challenges along the way. Perhaps unfairly, mistakes and problems that we would quickly forgive when the director came from the outside were not tolerated as easily because Michel was one of us (insiders should know better). And managers are invariably more direct and less diplomatic with people they know well.

But what ultimately makes our process work is that no matter who sits in the director's chair, the production is always a team effort. Like many of our best directors, Michel was quite generous about giving the cast lots of freedom to offer ideas and "cowrite" their parts rather than squeezing them into preconceived notions or barking orders. That made everyone in the show feel a deep sense of ownership in the final product. And he was not defensive about critiques during checkpoints, understanding that the Cirque way requires honest appraisals and an open sharing of ideas about how to make the product the best it can be.

A good example of that team effort can be seen in the development in one of *Kurios*'s most memorable scenes. For years, our creative team had been dreaming of an act that would take place completely upside down: everything would happen on the ceiling, with all the characters inverted. It's the kind of crazy challenge we love to dream about and then actually find a way to accomplish. Eager to finally try it out with *Kurios*, we invested a lot of money researching the details of how our artists could function under those circumstances (especially with the blood rushing to their heads!).

Eventually, we managed to create an act with five performers seated at a dinner table having what we called "the upside-down meal." When it came time to present it to Guy three weeks before opening night, the amazing ceiling structure we built attracted well-deserved attention—it was a thing to behold—but the act itself was mediocre at best, unable to live up to our expectations. Guy was merciless: "If you can't improve the artistic content of this thing, I'll remove it completely from the show."

A few days later, Guy returned to watch the rehearsals. The act had not improved. After spending so much time and effort developing this scene, everyone was crushed that it was apparently out. Then Jean-François Bouchard, our vice president of creation, offered an idea: "What if we tried to create a mirror effect?" he wondered. Why not create a replica of the dinner-party scene on the ground-level stage, with different cast members playing the same five characters dressed up the same way? One of them could stack up chairs on the table and climb up toward the ceiling. Meanwhile, another acrobat from the upside-down dinner party could do the same thing, stacking his chairs "up" (which is really down) until the two artists meet halfway in the middle of the space.

We tried it. The act worked beautifully, and it became one of the highlights of the show, taking the audience by surprise every time. When it opened in April of 2014, *Kurios* was a hit, and for years it was one of our most successful touring shows (much of its ticket sales were generated by word of mouth, always a good sign). Critics also loved it, calling it "kinetic, whimsical and astounding" (*Globe and Mail*), "the best Cirque du Soleil show in a long time" (*San Francisco Chronicle*), and "a dazzling, hyper-detailed, potent, quixotic and generally fantastic show" (*Chicago Tribune*).

Today we're extremely proud that Michel, whom I affectionately call "L'Enfant du Cirque," has worked his way up to become one of our top directors. After *Kurios*, he created *Séptimo Día—No Descansaré* ("Seventh Day—I Will Not Rest"), an arena show inspired by the music of the legendary Argentinian band Soda Stereo. Then he directed our exciting Disney collaboration, *Drawn to Life*, which was delayed by the pandemic but, as this book was going to press, was scheduled to open by the end of 2021.

An added benefit of developing talent from within is that success stories like Michel's inspire other employees to stay engaged and work hard, knowing they have a shot at the most coveted jobs that might otherwise go to people outside the company.

ESTABLISH AN OPEN CULTURE

Finding the best talent within your organization can be a challenge, so it's important to establish an open culture that encourages people to demonstrate their skills and ambitions. But how? At most firms, managers tell employees they are welcome—indeed, expected—to offer ideas about how to make the company or its products better. But simply saying "Come to us with brilliant ideas" won't produce much of value because it's too vague. Instead, offer specifics, like "We're looking for variations on Product X to roll out in two years when our existing customers will be craving something new." Prompts like that will get employees focused and make the process far more efficient.

One way I try to foster an open culture is by constantly reminding our employees that they can reach out to me anytime, on any subject, no matter their role. One day, I took a red-eye flight home after the painful process of shutting down a show in Las Vegas. When I got back to Montreal, I got an email from an employee who offered an idea for a new show at the resort we were vacating. His suggestion was not quite right and we had already lined up a replacement, but I was touched that, in the middle of a crisis over a failed show, he was already hitting me up with new ideas. I immediately thanked him and asked for more suggestions. That's a small example of the kind of open communication that can help identify the most enthusiastic and promising talent in your organization.

DON'T HIRE; CAST

Because Michel Laprise had worked in casting for many years, he was very familiar with our vast database of artists, which was a big help as he put together the stunning acrobatic acts of *Kurios*. He also made some great moves in assembling his team. Hiring the French costume designer Philippe Guillotel was a brilliant stroke. After doing a tremendous job on our *The Beatles LOVE* show, Philippe invented a series of astonishing outfits for *Kurios* that were a major factor in its success. The costume of one character, Mr. Microcosmos, was an enormous contraption with a door in the front of the stomach. When the door opens, the audience sees another character living inside: the painter-poetess Mini Lili, played by Antanina Satsura, who is three feet, two inches tall and weighs thirty-nine pounds (apparently one of the ten smallest people in the world). Set designer Stéphane Roy also made a huge impact on the show's steampunk theme with his dazzling retro-futuristic dreamscape.

Such skilled and daring artists are the key to Cirque's success. That's true for every firm, which makes the hiring process crucial. How best to approach the delicate task of finding the right talent? My advice is this: don't hire; cast.

Think of the movie business and how important it is to find just the right actor to play a part. Without Humphrey Bogart, *Casablanca* is just not the same film. The reverse is true when it comes to bad casting: if there is no chemistry between the leads in a romantic comedy, the film will be a disaster. Every company should look at hiring the same way—as casting decisions that can make or break your business.

When we cast, our goal is the same as yours should be—to recruit the best in the world. We want the top acrobats, jugglers, contortionists, aerialists, roller skaters, clowns, dancers, musicians, and more. But to succeed at Cirque—or at any company—the candidate must have more than just raw talent. He or she must also be a good fit with the company culture. For us, that means casting athletes who have an artistic streak and vice versa: artists who have the discipline of athletes.

Many of our cast members are world-class athletes, of course—gymnasts, high divers, synchronized swimmers, ice skaters, skateboarders, and more—and all have years of intense training behind them. But to be cast by Cirque, they must also enjoy performing, pleasing the crowd, and connecting with people emotionally. That's the magic ingredient that brings our shows to a whole new level.

Other cast members come from the arts world. They may be dancers, singers, or musicians accustomed to performing only once or twice per week. In that case, we have to train them like athletes so they can meet the heavy demands of our performance schedule. For permanent shows in Las Vegas and elsewhere, that means appearing in two shows per night for five consecutive nights every week (we encourage our artists to relax and have fun on their days off, but those who approach life as a nonstop party do not last long).

How can you find the talent you need? Establishing relationships with schools and other organizations that serve as a pipeline can be enormously helpful. About a third of our cast members come from sports organizations like the International Gymnastics Federation; a third from the arts (dancers, musicians, singers, mimes, and clowns); and another third from the circus world, especially schools in places like France, Germany, Ukraine, and Russia. Many of our artists come from the National Circus School in Montreal, cofounded by Cirque's first artistic director, Guy Caron, and conveniently located right next to our headquarters.

We are also constantly traveling the world scouting for great talent and expanding our networks. We evaluate video submissions, live performances, and competitions, and we run our own auditions. Our specialists examine technical abilities, physical readiness, and artistic qualities while making note of each candidate's work ethic, team spirit, and ability to not only follow directions but come up with their own creative ideas as we develop the characters in a show.

The best of the best are brought to our Montreal headquarters, where they undergo a training period that can last anywhere from one month to six months, depending on the show, how experienced they are, and how many new skills they need to learn. We start with a fitness evaluation and then move on to physical and artistic training. We like to push them out of their comfort zone to see what they are capable of while adhering to rigorous safety standards. Those who pass our program are gradually integrated into the cast of one of our touring or permanent shows.

Today, we have amassed an enormous database of 130,000 performers from around the world that we tap into whenever a need arises. Our standards are so high that only about 10 percent of those are seriously considered for a Cirque production, but we keep an eye on the others for signs of progress.

I recently asked our vice president for casting and performance, Bernard Petiot, to define what it takes to become a Cirque performer. He said, "These people are so passionate, and have committed themselves so deeply to develop their skills, that you watch them and say, 'How the hell did they learn to do that?!' That's what makes them special. They are never satisfied and are constantly pushing themselves to be better." That sounds like a great definition of an ideal employee in any industry: people who constantly drive themselves to improve and find more creative ways to do their jobs.

A good example of that kind of person is Ray Wold, one of Cirque's more unusual performers. As he was coming up in the circus world, Ray said, he was never satisfied with the usual acts—riding a unicycle, juggling knives and machetes, breathing fire. He wanted a new trick that would make him stand out, so he began setting himself on fire.

Ray's spectacular act attracted our scouts when he performed at a prestigious circus festival in Monte Carlo in 1997, just as we were putting together our Las Vegas water show, *O*. Our casting people liked the idea of blending fire with water and thought the image of a man who bursts into flames would be perfect for the surreal, dreamy atmosphere of our new production.

For more than two decades, our daring burning clown has put on a fire-resistant Kevlar suit and hat saturated with Coleman camping fuel. Ray saunters onto the stage looking like a hobo, sits down in a chair, and begins casually reading a newspaper, oblivious to the fact that one of his shoes has caught fire. The conflagration soon spreads to his legs and arms until he is completely engulfed in flames. All the while, he calmly continues reading. Fortunately, most of his skin is covered and his face is protected by the upturned lapel of his jacket, his hunched shoulders, and simple clown greasepaint. About three minutes later—as the temperature outside his suit reaches a staggering nine hundred degrees—he shuffles offstage. There, a crew wraps him up in blankets that extinguish the fire.

Over the years, Ray has gotten singed hair and blisters but never a single serious injury during his performances in *O*. Incredibly, he has never missed a show.

For most people, it's beyond belief that someone would voluntarily light himself on fire, night after night. But Ray is motivated by the same drive that pushes many high achievers. "So many people are trying to be entertainers," he once told an interviewer. "They try to take the easy road and copy what others are doing. To be original, to be unique, that's the hardest road. The only thing that was really in my mind was how to entertain people and be a success. I was willing to do just about anything."

When you cast employees with that kind of dedication, managing them is relatively easy. You give them the tools they need to perform—and, in our case, make sure they don't hurt themselves—and then leave them alone to indulge their passion and work their magic. In my experience, no manager can push truly dedicated employees harder than they push themselves when they are doing something they love.

In the end, our casting philosophy boils down to looking for the best artist for every show. That may sound like common sense, but I'm not sure that traditional companies follow that rule when posting an opening in finance, human resources, or information technology. They are often so eager to fill the position that they rush the process. Entertainment companies have deadlines, too, but we tend to be less inclined to throw just anybody into a role. The public nature of what we do quickly reveals how well we chose our artists. Every company can approach their own casting process the same way.

KEEP AN OPEN MIND

Our casting approach can also be applied to business partnerships. Choosing partners who truly understand your company and its culture can lead to breakthroughs you may never have thought possible. Choosing badly, on the other hand, can make your life a nightmare.

Sometimes it can be hard to tell the difference at first. When Guy and I first met Daniel Chávez Morán in early 2010, we didn't know how seriously to take this fiftysomething engineer/businessman with long hair who came to visit us wearing a T-shirt and jeans. He wanted to invite us to his resorts in Mexico, where he hoped to create a Cirque du Soleil theme park.

The idea of a theme park had always been both intriguing and problematic for us. We had considered it many times before and kept encountering the same obstacle—how to make it different from all the other amusement parks out there? Cirque's brand is so unique that our fans would expect something truly astonishing and off-the-wall, but none of our ideas ever rose to that level. We didn't want to simply imitate Disney or Six Flags. Our explorations *did* generate some interesting ideas, but they were all too crazy and impractical to fit the needs of a modern theme park.

So we dragged our feet for a long time, unable to see how a partnership with Daniel would amount to anything. But he was so insistent and gracious and intelligent that Guy and I agreed to fly to visit two of his resorts, in Riviera Maya and Puerto Vallarta, Mexico. Instantly, we were glad we did. The landscaping was beautiful and innovative and his passion for preserving the environment was clear and powerful. The buildings were spotless, and he had built his own laboratory to test the water to make sure no visitors got sick. Today, his company, Grupo Vidanta, has a chain of hotels and golf courses throughout Latin America, from Medellín to Acapulco, and is one of the region's largest employers. The company is ethical and compassionate, regularly making the list of Best Companies to Work for in Mexico, and Daniel is a successful, wealthy man with a stellar reputation.

Still, we could not get past the theme park problems, and it was hard to find other projects we could work on together. A big resident show at one of his resorts was not likely to work because they did not have the foot traffic to support it. Daniel, it seemed, was destined to remain an admired friend and nothing more.

But creativity is a magical and elusive thing. Sometimes, the most you can do is establish conditions for it to flower and hope for the best. That's what Daniel and I were doing over dinner one night in Montreal. An important ingredient was the bottle of his favorite vintage, Château Lafite Rothschild, that we were both enjoying. As the wine and conversation flowed, I said, "Daniel, you're great and I love your resorts and your whole business, but it will take too long to dream up and build a theme park. Why can't we do something else, something we could put together faster?"

As we talked, I thought about his beautiful resorts and the sensory indulgence they offered with excellent food and wine and stunning natural scenery. Without thinking, I blurted out, "How about a dinner show?"

Daniel did not hesitate. "Yes, let's do it!"

Joyà, our first dinner show, and our first permanent production in Latin America, opened in Riviera Maya, just south of Cancún, in November of 2014. Daniel outdid himself with the construction of the theater in a remote jungle location. To preserve the natural habitat, a wooden walkway leading to the theater was built aboveground, allowing animals to pass underneath. The magnificent landscaping included pools of water, coral rocks, and a waterfall. Guests can have drinks and food at a nearby bar and grill or inside the theater at their tables starting an hour before showtime (the menu itself is edible). *Joyà*, our first North American show to reopen after the pandemic, is a thrilling, immersive experience that places the crowd just a few feet away from the performers; some acts even extend out into the audience.

At six hundred seats, our dinner theater in Riviera Maya is less than half the size of our usual resident productions, creating a whole new category of shows for us. Now we are planning a new dinner show at another of Daniel's resorts, in Nuevo Vallarta, just north of Puerto Vallarta on Mexico's Pacific coast. *Joyà* also provided the impetus for a series of shows aboard cruise ships called Cirque du Soleil at Sea in partnership with MSC Cruises, the world's largest privately owned cruise line. Though each of these productions are relatively small, in the aggregate they add up to a significant revenue stream. (Our partnership with Daniel also led to a new show celebrating Mexican culture; 2016's *Luzia* quickly became one of our most popular touring productions.)

None of this would have been possible had we given up during our talks with Daniel. It was a great lesson in keeping an open mind. At creative companies, you never know where the next great idea might come from.

CREATE "INNOVATION CELLS"

Companies our size often pass up the chance to develop smaller products and services, feeling that they are not worth the time. But *Joyà* taught us that going small can pay off in many ways— not only in profitability, but also in developing creative talent. Until our foray into Mexico, our "special events" division stuck mostly to one-off shows for sponsors looking to make a splash with a single event featuring Cirque du Soleil acts. *Joyà* made us realize that our special-events directors were well suited for this new category of smaller shows. While better-known directors might have turned their noses up at doing a dinner show or a Cirque du Soleil at Sea production, our younger directors saw them as an exciting promotion that offered them a chance to show what they could do.

Our special-events division is just one example of what I call "innovation cells" that companies can establish to nurture creativity within their organization. Forget the traditional pyramid structure—that tends to stifle experimentation. Employees need smaller, more intimate groups to express themselves and play around with new ideas in a supportive environment.

In fact, each show we produce is created by an autonomous group, or cell, made up of artists who are singularly focused on that show. That's why we could grow so large without compromising quality. We don't act like a big company. Nobody is stretched too thin by working on multiple productions, because there is very little overlap between these cells. Most of our creators have nothing to do but make their show the best it can be.

Several innovation cells at Cirque are devoted to another crucial aspect of a creative culture that companies ignore to their own detriment: research and development.

INVEST IN R&D

Despite our growth over the years, Cirque is still too small to afford the kind of basic research that national governments or giant firms like Apple or Google routinely engage in—deep scientific inquiries that may not yield practical results for years or decades (if ever). But we can pursue applied research that tries to solve the type of real-world problems we face daily. No, it's not cheap, but in today's hypercompetitive global economy, I am convinced that it's critical to devote funds and staff to research and development, whether you are a small firm trying to carve out a market or a large one hoping to keep your competitive advantage.

To maintain our hard-won place on the cutting edge of live entertainment, we have established several cells devoted exclusively to R and D. One is our Trends Group, a team of three full-time employees who search the world for new ideas and talents in all cultural sectors: music, fashion, architecture, theater, film, games, and more. Every three or four months, they present our creative teams with the treasures they have discovered, and we begin exploring how they might be used in a show.

Another program, the Creative Watch, encourages all our employees to bring to the Trends Group anything strikingly original or intriguing they have come across that we might feature in a production. That's become a great way to make every member of our team—from accountants to custodians—feel part of the creative process, and it helps to keep them more fully engaged in their jobs.

The Trends Group and Creative Watch are part of a larger research department we call C-Lab that sifts through hundreds of ideas and selects a few major projects per year to focus on—everything from new stage technology to biomechanical breakthroughs that reduce injuries to our artists. C-Lab members stay in constant contact with show producers to see if their lab innovations can be used in an upcoming show—a new fabric that might work better for costumes with lights, for example. One exciting innovation, developed with Microsoft, is called HoloLens. It's a pair of augmented-reality smartglasses that allows our directors to see what the entire stage will look like before it's even built. The HoloLens allows us to experiment with every aspect of the set—characters, lighting, props, rigging—and visualize a variety of layouts, making production planning far more creative and efficient.

It doesn't do any good to invest in such research efforts, however, if employees don't buy in. That's why I am constantly looking for ways to remind our team that *everyone* should play an active role in keeping our place on the vanguard of entertainment. One day, one of Cirque's creative directors, Jean-François Bouchard, came into my office and said, "Daniel, there's a professor in Switzerland who has invented this amazing new type of drone. It has highly advanced fail-safe algorithms that could work very well within complex ecosystems of stage automation like ours. Really phenomenal."

I narrowed my gaze and said sternly, "What are you doing in my office?"

"What?" he said. "I thought you'd want to hear about—"

"I love your idea. But why are we sitting here talking about it? Run to the airport and go to Switzerland. I want to see those drones!"

I was having fun with Jean-François for a reason: I knew that word of our meeting would spread, and I wanted to send a signal to our employees that we'll do whatever it takes to discover new ideas.

Jean-François did fly to Zurich, and we developed those amazing drones together with the distinguished professor Raffaello D'Andrea. We used them in our 2016 Broadway show *Paramour*, which moved to Hamburg three years later and ran until it became a casualty of the pandemic. In one act, a swarm of colorful lampshades—looking like glowing, circular hatboxes—floated above the performers. The audience assumed they were hanging by wires from the ceiling. But when characters moved their arms over them, it became clear that they were moving independently. It's a brilliant trick we may use in other productions.

WORK WITH CREATIVE LEADERS

Sometimes maintaining a creative edge requires another tactic not used often enough: collaborating with leaders in your field who can inspire your team to rise to even greater heights.

That's what happened with our 2015 arena-touring show *Toruk—The First Flight*, when we had the honor of working with a giant in the entertainment world. It all happened by a crazy stroke of good fortune. I was in Los Angeles for the premiere of one of our touring shows when Julie Payette—the same Canadian astronaut who encouraged Guy to make his trip to outer space—came up to say hello.

"What are you doing early tomorrow morning?" Julie asked as I sipped champagne.

"Not sure," I said. "Why?"

"I'm meeting with James Cameron. Would you like to join me?"

Would I? The meeting was scheduled for 8:00 a.m., and it was getting late. I thanked Julie profusely and rushed off to find my wife, the photographer Emmanuelle Dupérré.

"Stop drinking, Emmanuelle," I said, taking her glass. "We're leaving."

"But we're having a good time!" she protested. "What's the matter? Is something wrong?"

"No, no, no, we're going to meet James Cameron first thing tomorrow morning."

She looked at me, puzzled, and said, "I think you've had too much champagne!"

The next morning, we arrived at James Cameron's studio, right on time, and Julie introduced us. He had no idea we were coming but seemed genuinely happy to see us. "Let me show you the costumes and makeup for my latest film because you'll see a bit of Cirque du Soleil in there," he said. "I'm a big fan—always very inspired by what you guys are doing."

He showed us around the studio where he was practically living, working eighteen hours a day and catching a few hours of sleep each night on a small makeshift bed. I thought we would spend ten minutes exchanging pleasantries and then leave him alone to work. But despite his crazy schedule as he raced to finish the movie, James spent more than an hour with us, demonstrating his complex motion-capture and 3D technology and sharing footage of his astonishing film. I was touched by his dedication to his work and his generosity toward a stranger.

"You know what?" he said as we exchanged goodbyes. "When I finish this gig, I'd love to meet with you again and sit down to see what we might do together."

This "gig," as he called it, was none other than *Avatar*, which would become the highest-grossing film in history (at the time), eclipsing the record set by his earlier Oscar winner, *Titanic*.

A few months later, James came to visit us in Montreal and was blown away by our headquarters. What I was most taken by was his relentless curiosity—about costume design, makeup, lighting, stage technology, and more. He wanted to know every detail about *everything*. "This place is so much fun," he said. "I want to work here!"

Afterward, at dinner at Guy's house with plenty of wine, we talked about doing a show together based on *Avatar*. We had a fantastic time. When it was over, he stood up and said, "I'm ready to rock!"

Negotiating with 20th Century Fox for the rights to *Avatar* was a challenge, but James had done so much for the studio that they were eager to accommodate his wishes. James would not direct the show himself—that was handled by the talented duo Michel Lemieux and Victor Pilon—but he did serve an important role as creative consultant to help guide us.

A project like this could have been a nightmare if James had been one of those artists who cannot entrust their baby to anyone else. That often happens with creators who feel deeply attached to their work. But James had a powerfully constructive impact on our team. Rather than reining us in, he inspired us to go further than Cirque had ever gone before. More than anything else, we wanted to impress him.

Our creative team started off by becoming immersed in the intricate world of *Avatar*, which James had spent fifteen years inventing. We used the same choreographer and linguist who worked on the film to make sure our performers moved and spoke like the indigenous Na'vi people of Pandora. That background work was far more important than any specific direction James could offer us because it allowed us to work from the authentic core of his fantastical world. All our inspiration came from that hallowed place.

As we developed the show, it became so massive and technically complex that we realized it would not work in a typical big-top tent. So we set up a tour in large sports arenas, as we often do with productions that are too big for tents but don't require the construction of an entire theater. One major innovation was the installation of forty projectors on the ceiling that splashed images on the floor of the stage, sometimes extending out to the audience, that completely transformed the scene and produced astonishing effects like rushing water or flowing lava, augmented by realistic sound effects (we would later use such projectors in other productions, including our 2017 ice show, *Crystal*). Our version of Pandora was so deeply immersive—forests, flowers, rocks, wild animals, birds, the Na'vi people—that even our performers fell under its spell. As Gabriel Christo, who played the character Ralu, put it, "As I'm in there, everything fades away. All I see is Pandora."

Toruk—The First Flight was a huge hit when it premiered in December of 2015 at the 14,000-seat CenturyLink Center in Bossier City, Louisiana. Audiences were stunned to see the *Avatar* film brought to physical life with such an original interpretation.

Like *The Beatles LOVE* and *Michael Jackson ONE*, we had put our own unique spin on a cultural icon. *Avatar* and Cirque, it turns out, were a match made in heaven.

"I've always said that Cirque du Soleil is about a celebration of human physicality and human excellence," James said later. "Part of the Na'vi culture is about being alive in your own body and being alive as part of a community, part of a group of people. And when you see the Cirque performers working, with perfect synchronization, these amazing kind of group acrobatics, that's a very Na'vi concept."

We could never have produced a show of *Toruk*'s magnitude without partnering with a genius like James. Which raises an intriguing question for every company: Who is the James Cameron of your industry? Who in your field inspires you the most? Why not make a list of those names and brainstorm ways to connect with them? You never know how receptive they might be to your brand—whether corporate or personal—and how much their encouragement and direction might lead you to new creative heights. If you can't connect or the chemistry is not right, no problem. Just go to the next name on your list until something clicks. My hunch is that you'll be glad you did.

As we were developing *Toruk*, despite the usual jitters, we had a strong sense that our hot streak was intact. Together with *Michael Jackson ONE*, *Kurios*, and *Joyà*, we felt confident that we had our fourth groundbreaking hit in three years. Life was good, but ease and comfort are not among the hallmarks of any creative company—and certainly not part of our culture. Turbulence and upheaval are more the norm, and they returned to our Montreal headquarters with a vengeance one day when Guy surprised us with sobering news: after more than thirty years at Cirque du Soleil, he was ready to sell the company.

CHAPTER 6

SHOW COMES BEFORE BUSINESS

For years, Guy Laliberté had been talking about one day sell-ing a majority stake in the company he cofounded back in 1984. But it was just that—talk—until June of 2014, when he called a meeting with me and our chief financial officer at the time, Robert Blain, and told us he was finally ready to pull the trigger.

By then, we knew his reasoning well: Guy's main goal, from the beginning, was to travel the world, put on shows, and have fun. As the company grew, he kept looking for ways to lighten his load of responsibilities, craving a life with as much adventure and freedom as possible. That's why he asked me to take over day-to-day management as CEO in 2006, when he stepped back into the role of creative guide, and why he blasted off into outer space three years later. Now he felt it was time to transfer Cirque to new owners who could bring the company to the next level.

"Selling is the best option for Cirque," Guy told me. "It's also best for me, so I can capitalize on thirty years of investing my life into this company." He never wanted to be the kind of entre-preneur who could not let go of his creation and let it grow big and strong without him. "I have many other dreams," he said. "Personal dreams, family dreams, entrepreneurial dreams to challenge myself with. This feels like the right time."

MAINTAIN STABILITY IN TIMES OF CHANGE

Robert and I were not exactly surprised, but it was still hard to hear Guy say those words. For thirty years, he had been the heart and soul of the company—the father of our close-knit Cirque family—and it was nearly impossible to imagine life without him. Robert, in fact, immediately told Guy he would prefer to leave Cirque and come work for him in a private capacity. Later, that's exactly what he did.

Then Guy looked at me. "What are you going to do?"

I did not hesitate: "I am staying."

This was not technically true, of course. Whether I stayed or not would be up to our new owners, not me. And even if they did want me, I wasn't sure that I'd want to work with them, depending on who it was. But during this time of uncertainty and upheaval, it seemed important to maintain stability within the organization by declaring my intention to stay.

I also had some goals of my own. "First, I want to help you sell the company and strike a deal that you will be very happy with," I told Guy. "Second, I hope you won't be too mad at me when I grow this company—and its market value—much bigger than it is right now."

Guy and Robert laughed, enjoying my chutzpah. We all knew that smart new owners could help Cirque reach its true potential, and I was excited to help that process along. Since Guy planned to retain a small share of the company, any growth we achieved would benefit him as well. "Okay," he said with a grin. "We'll see."

As word of the impending sale began to circulate, our employees naturally began to worry. The most pessimistic wondered if this would be the end of Cirque du Soleil as we knew it. So it was very important for me to keep telling our people, every chance I got, "I'm staying. And if I'm staying, *you're* staying."

I also reminded them of my philosophy of show business: "The word *show* comes first for a reason. If you don't have a good show, you don't *have* a business." So I would do everything in my power, I assured them, to make sure our new owners did not interfere with the creative process. Our talks seemed to have a calming effect on our staff.

As we began the search for a new owner, I let people know that only three players would be involved in the process: Guy, Robert, and me. "I don't want you to spend another moment thinking about this," I told our employees. "Just continue doing your job as usual, as if nothing has changed. Because when this is over, the only changes will be positive. We will be exactly the same company but with more capital to invest in producing spectacular shows."

Of course, people still gossiped about rumors or news they had heard. But for the most part, they kept the faith, focusing on their work so well that we successfully opened *Joyà* in November of 2014 and *Toruk* the following year. Had we brought our senior executives into the early stages of the search process and solicited input from around the organization about the various buyer candidates, it would have been hard to imagine people getting anything done. I've seen that happen at other companies, and it's not a pretty sight. At worst, such distractions can threaten the very viability of the firm.

That's why maintaining stability during times of change is so important—especially for creative firms because they tend to take on more risks and have more potential for disruption than a traditional company. In a global economy beset by technological change, companies are bought and sold so frequently that our situation was hardly unusual. But the distraction an organization faces does not have to be as big as being sold to a new owner. It might be searching for a new CEO, moving to a new headquarters, or reorganizing a department. No matter what causes the tumult, it's critical to put as few people in charge of the transition as possible so business can continue as usual.

Even body language is important to keep the company on an even keel. People often accuse business leaders of being introverted and not showing their feelings often enough. That's true, but I also believe it's crucial to maintain some distance at certain moments and not let one's emotions influence decisions. Without even realizing it, you can send the wrong signal through your choice of language, attitude, or even physical posture. In delicate circumstances, employees are searching for any hint of something awry. To ride through the turbulence without flinching, the captain must stay calm and relaxed, with both hands firmly on the wheel.

ASSOCIATE WITH CLASS ACTS

Our first move was to hire Goldman Sachs to lead the search for a buyer. My job as CEO was to submit detailed presentations to all potential suitors. For several months, my schedule was out of control. Within a few hours' notice, I had to be available to take questions from prospective buyers on the phone or race to a meeting. At first, fifty-four companies showed interest. We made countless presentations, showcasing the company in the best possible light, and answered the same questions dozens of times. We narrowed the list down to thirty-two candidates, then eighteen, then nine. It was quite a pressure cooker. We felt like every potential buyer was decoding and analyzing our every word and gesture.

The tension increased when we reached the stage of presenting to eight top contenders. Until then, I had led all the presentations along with Robert. The next round, over eight full days, required the presence of ten members of senior management trained to make such pitches and answer all manner of questions. That was followed by the dozens of phone calls we received with yet more questions. Eventually, we narrowed our list to three finalists: a Chinese group, a joint American-European group, and an intriguing partnership between the private equity firm TPG Capital of San Francisco and the conglomerate Fosun International of Shanghai.

We also knew the giant Quebec pension fund Caisse de dépôt et placement du Québec would probably get involved. As soon as it learned that Cirque was for sale, Caisse told Goldman Sachs, "Regardless of who buys a majority of the company, we would like a 10 percent stake so we will have a voice in keeping Cirque, and all its jobs, right here in Quebec." Having in our corner such a powerful institutional investor, with hundreds of billions of Canadian dollars under management, was very reassuring to our staff members who wanted to stay in Montreal.

As we negotiated with the final three, our advisers felt things were not moving along fast enough. So they suggested I book a trip to Hong Kong to meet the Chinese group, hoping it would light a fire under the other two candidates. It worked. I had not even reached the airport when TPG/Fosun requested a meeting as soon as I arrived there. When my flight landed, I had barely enough time to rush to the hotel and shower before I was due at a reception hosted by Fosun. It was an impressive gathering on the rooftop of a hotel with breathtaking views of the bustling city of Hong Kong.

I expected to be the center of attention at this event. Instead, I felt lost in the crowd of guests, who all knew each other from the local business community. That's the strange thing about being a Westerner in China and its territories. In business settings, if you don't have deep personal relationships—what the Chinese call *guanxi*—you quickly become the odd person out. That's where I was at the party, feeling lonely and isolated at the very moment I was supposed to be actively closing in on a deal.

Then something remarkable happened: I recognized Silas Chou, a well-known Hong Kong businessman. I knew Silas through his partner in the fashion industry, Lawrence Stroll, a Canadian billionaire who knew Guy through the international car-racing circuit. I rushed to Silas as if my life depended on it. As we exchanged warm greetings, the dynamics of the party changed instantly. Within minutes, I was transformed from a suspicious stranger into a respected and credible businessman, a force to be reckoned with. Thanks to Silas, I was able to establish excellent relationships with the people of Fosun. In turn, Silas vouched for Fosun, saying we would make a great team. By the end of the evening, I felt sure this company could be a tremendous partner to help open the doors to China.

I do not believe the cliché "It's not what you know, it's who you know." Expertise, hard work, and tenacity are still the foundations of business success, in my view. But there is no doubt—especially in a place like China—that the type of people you associate with can have a huge impact on your career. Silas Chou has always been a class act, and that's a big reason why I have always looked for ways to get to know him better. I could never have predicted, of course, that someday he would magically appear at a party to change the trajectory of a big business deal.

But I've always had faith that good things happen when you surround yourself with quality people.

The opposite is also true. Getting in deep with disreputable people can only come back to haunt you. That's why I tend to stay far away from smooth talkers and con artists, even when there's a significant potential upside. I was reminded of this principle over the next two days when I spent time with the Chinese group I had originally flown to Hong Kong to see. While the organization itself was highly professional, courteous, and ethical, their advisers were not. During my short stay, they tried to get me to drink too much so I would reveal privileged information. They were juvenile, irritating, and in constant sales mode. Just before I left, they took me aside and told me I would become very rich if I chose them—not seeming to understand that I wasn't even the owner. Their behavior gave me every reason to advise Guy that they would not be a good match.

ADMIT YOUR WEAKNESSES

By contrast, the TPG/Fosun group won me over. TPG partners Jim Coulter, David Bonderman, and David Trujillo were smart and serious and seemed to genuinely want to protect the creative spirit that had fueled Cirque's ascent. Based in the San Francisco Bay Area, they also had a deep involvement in Silicon Valley that could help us better use social media to market Cirque and collaborate with industry leaders like Facebook, Google, and Twitter. TPG was especially impressed that our Net Promoter Score—a measure of customer loyalty—exceeded that of nearly every brand on the market. "Delivering what Cirque delivers around the world to millions of viewers every year is really an incredibly difficult thing," Coulter told an interviewer later. "So watching them do that, and do it very well, has really been a learning experience for me." Fosun, meanwhile, led by the brilliant and influential billionaire chairman Guo Guangchang—known by some as the Warren Buffett of China—already had significant entertainment assets and would give us a solid foothold in the enormous Chinese market.

It was sobering to realize that TPG/Fosun was the only finalist I would feel comfortable working for. But I would not be choosing our next owners. That was up to Guy. Nor could I, in good conscience, even attempt to influence his decision. Negotiating for Cirque against my future employer was a clear conflict of interest. Plus, Guy and I had conflicting goals: he wanted to maximize his return, and I wanted the buyer who would be the best fit for the company. So I had little choice but to bow out of the final negotiations and observe from the sidelines. From then on, Goldman Sachs and Guy's personal adviser were in charge.

Watching the process that would determine my future at Cirque—whose employees felt like members of my own family—was nerve-racking. So I was ecstatic when the highest bidder turned out to be the TPG group. For a total bid of 1.5 billion US dollars, TPG received 55 percent of the company; Fosun had 25 percent; Caisse de dépôt et placement du Québec got a 10 percent stake; and Guy retained the final 10 percent. It was a highly leveraged deal—the group borrowed $700 million to complete the transaction—but the banks had no problem approving the loans because our profit margins were so healthy and prospects for continued international growth remained quite strong, especially in China.

I was relieved when the new owners asked me to stay on. Despite the usual apprehensions about working for a new boss, I was happy to say yes and get back to work growing the company. Guy agreed to remain an informal presence at Cirque, available for advice on matters large and small, and we were happy that we would still have access to his deep expertise. (We even kept Guy's office as a symbol of his continued involvement, though he rarely used it.)

Going through the acquisition process was a humbling experience. Having each suitor probe your company in such minute detail gives you a clear picture of not only your strengths but also your weaknesses. In that situation, getting defensive—though understandable—is not helpful. Painful as it can be, the best approach is to admit your problems quickly and figure out how to fix them. I was glad to have lots of assistance in making the necessary changes from a board of directors loaded with talent. As I told them often, my attitude is "I never turn down help."

One of our biggest issues was that we were not set up like a modern corporation in key areas like accounting, executive staffing, and business development. So we created a new financial reporting system, beefed up our data analytics, and made new hires in finance, operations, marketing, and human resources. After fifteen years of collaborating with Guy in an informal environment, I would now be working for a more corporate organization—but one I vowed would still have all the quirkiness of the original.

Another weakness was in social media. As part of its analysis of the company, TPG arranged for focus groups of millennials to come to our shows and answer survey questions. These young adults loved the experience, but when asked why they'd never been to a Cirque show before, they said, "Because they never talk to us." In other words, we were not showing up in the digital neighborhoods they hung out in. Partly that was by design. Like an experienced magician, Guy was never a big fan of pulling back the curtain to reveal the secrets behind our acts. But today, sharing behind-the-scenes content online is crucial to establishing lasting relationships with new generations of ticket buyers.

Using platforms like Facebook, Twitter, YouTube, and Instagram, we began sharing content about performances, artists, backstage activities, our creative process, and life on tour. Our fans couldn't get enough of it. We realized that social media was very similar to old-fashioned word of mouth, which had always driven our ticket sales, far more than traditional advertising. The results were striking. We registered a 25 percent increase in millennials who considered the Cirque du Soleil brand relevant. In North America and Europe, our brand awareness increased from 85 percent to fully 95 percent. By 2017, we had more than ten million social media followers while a content strategy fueled by our fans called #CirqueWay reached more than one billion people.

That's the thing about admitting your weaknesses. It can be embarrassing at first, but when you act upon that information, it can make you so much stronger in the long run.

GROW BY LEVERAGING YOUR STRENGTHS

Guy was never a big fan of growing through acquisitions, but TPG understood that buying smaller firms could be a great way for us to take advantage of efficiencies of scale without endangering our core business. But we couldn't buy just any company. The key was finding those with a similar business model who shared our values, core competence, and overall brand strategy.

That's not to say that some companies can't grow effectively by expanding into new areas unrelated to their main business—"conglomerate diversification," in corporate jargon. Big firms from Berkshire Hathaway to Tata Group to Virgin Group have done so quite successfully. But it's not an easy strategy to execute well, and it carries considerable risk. Look no further than Coca-Cola's failed foray into the wine business and Kodak's short-lived move into pharmaceuticals. It's an especially difficult act to pull off for creative companies with a strong culture that may not blend well with firms from entirely different industries. In chapter 2, I talked about how the proposed Complex Cirque project at Battersea in London would have been a disaster for us because we are not a real-estate firm and have no expertise in that area.

As we discussed acquisition plans with TPG, I was glad to see we all agreed to stick with live-entertainment companies whose outlook and creative culture were similar to ours. That's why the Blue Man Group was so enticing when we discovered it was for sale. Founded in 1987 in Manhattan's Lower East Side, the blue men were similar to Cirque in many ways: both began as street performers in the 1980s and created an original form of entertainment; in both cases, the show—rather than the performers—is the star; both used popular and obscure music, art, and movement in fresh and surprising ways. Already international in scope, Blue Man Group had permanent shows in Las Vegas, Boston, Chicago, Orlando, New York, and Berlin and toured around the world.

When we bought Blue Man Group in 2017, both companies benefited from robust synergies. Though Cirque's distribution strength is not nearly as appreciated as its creative output, we were the only entertainment company in the world that toured in more than 450 cities on nearly every continent. That made a huge impact on Blue Man Group's ability to expand globally, and it inspired us to acquire two more companies over the next two years: VStar Entertainment Group, which produces family touring shows based on *PAW Patrol, Trolls,* and others; and The Works Entertainment, producers of The Illusionists magic shows. Now when we go into a city like London, we can produce shows for both Cirque and our various subsidiaries, each one appealing to different audiences. Each acquisition allows us to efficiently deploy Cirque's vast live-entertainment touring operation.

After we acquired VStar, I met with the company's employees and realized that we offered them something else: our reputation. When a company is sold, its staff can be seized by paralyzing feelings of insecurity. With VStar, it was quite the opposite. Our reputation as a creative organization that treats its artists well made our new employees happy to be associated with our brand. It also put them in a constructive frame of mind when dealing with various challenges, like how to preserve their firm's character and agility while being owned by a larger company.

Buying each of these companies was part of TPG's strategy to grow quickly, investing $100 million per year in new shows and acquisitions. Its goal was the same as nearly every private-equity company: to create more value and then sell for a profit within five to seven years. While these investment firms often get a bad rap in the press—especially when they heartlessly impose layoffs to maximize their gains—these growth initiatives have been a blessing for us, providing a big influx of resources so we can produce more shows. After all, that's what we do, and it's what makes us happy. Suddenly, we had more creators dreaming up new shows, more artists working, more tours and resident productions, and more thrilled audiences around the world. We were like a kid in a candy store.

With any change of ownership, there's always a danger that the new bosses will think they know your business better than you do and start telling you what to do. It's something our employees were very concerned about in April of 2015 when Guy announced we were being sold to the TPG group. Worries raced through our headquarters and backstage at shows: "Will we lose our soul? Will we stay in Montreal? Will we even want to work here anymore?" Addressing those fears instantly became my top priority.

PROTECT THE CREATORS

It's natural for people on the financial side of any company to try to influence the creation of products or services. They might commission marketing studies or develop their own opinions about what will or won't sell. This is where many companies go awry, especially after some initial success. Suits start making decisions instead of letting the creative teams work without interference.

This dynamic is why Guy always steadfastly refused to discuss financial matters with our employees. He wanted to keep them focused on their work and let their imaginations roam free without worry. We had to temporarily break that rule when he decided to sell the company in the interest of keeping everyone informed. This news created considerable tension, as expected, and I was as nervous as anyone about whether the new owners would understand and protect our magical culture—even after I told TPG, in no uncertain terms, that it must leave the creative side alone.

Fortunately, they understood from the beginning that even when spending $40 million to $50 million developing a new show, they had to leave the dreaming to the dreamers. So, while we did make big changes in executive leadership on the business side, our creative team was kept fully intact after the sale. And I made it clear that imposing layers of bureaucracy would slow down our creative process. As I told people from administrative services, "Leave the show creators alone—I want them to be 100 percent focused on their work, not worrying about some new HR policy. I want them to eat, breathe, and sleep their new shows."

Private-equity firms don't always agree to be so hands-off after making a purchase, but TPG felt that Cirque's creative team had earned its autonomy with its spectacular track record. Once the shock of having a new owner subsided, our creators were able to forget about who was in charge and focus on what they love doing most of all: inventing new shows.

EXPLOIT LESSONS LEARNED

In our business, nothing tells employees that the company is thriving more than the sight of artists in the studio creating their imaginary worlds, the sounds of laughter and music bouncing off the walls. That was the atmosphere at headquarters after the sale of Cirque was formally completed in July of 2015. With new owners pouring substantial resources into our operation, we premiered two new productions in April of 2016 (the touring *Luzia* and *Paramour* on Broadway) and geared up for three more in 2017—the first time we had produced so many shows since the wake of the Great Recession.

By then, Cirque was well into its fourth decade. As we settled into a rhythm, it occurred to me that maturity can be a wonderful thing: you can exploit your hard-won experience to avoid the mistakes of youth and concentrate fully on executing your vision.

The lessons we learned along the way, each described in previous chapters of this book, helped guide us forward:

- The long journey of creating *The Beatles LOVE* a decade earlier—not to mention two hit Michael Jackson shows—gave us the confidence to create our own original interpretation of another iconic musical act, the Argentinian pop group Soda Stereo. *Séptimo Día—No Descansaré*, directed by Michel Laprise, toured sold-out arenas full of rapturous fans throughout Latin America from March 2017 to September of the following year.

- The mistake we made with *Criss Angel Believe* and *Banana Shpeel*—not using enough acrobatics—almost derailed us again when our new production, *Volta*, hurtled toward its Montreal premiere in April of 2017. The concept was a show based on extreme sports—bicycle motocross, roller skates, unicycles—but we got too carried away with the story at the expense of the spectacular acts our audience expects. Our chief creative officer, Diane Quinn, came to the rescue at the last minute and brought acrobatics front and center. *Volta* opened with a bang, much to our relief, and remained a big draw on tour.

- Sometimes a show's troubles can be traced to a flawed mandate—like *Viva Elvis*, with its trite and outdated approach as a stage biography of a pop star. Our first ice show, *Crystal*, by contrast, became a huge success in 2017 and beyond in large part because the mandate was so clear and compelling: just as *O* was an acrobatic production based on water, *Crystal* would be based on ice. With dazzling acts and pulsing with the lighting innovations of *Toruk*, *Crystal* became so popular on its global arena tour that we created a second ice production, *Axel*, two years later.

In 2018, we paused to catch our breath, creating just one new show, *Bazzar*, our first foray into India. Like our Mexican dinner show *Joyà* and Cirque du Soleil at Sea on cruise ships, *Bazzar* was a more intimate affair. Performed in a tent much smaller than our usual big top, it also had a lower budget and ticket price. *Bazzar* represented another lesson well learned: less extravagant productions can still reach a significant audience that we might otherwise miss. To use a baseball metaphor, why rely solely on home runs when you can also win by hitting singles?

By 2019, we were ready for the most ambitious run in our history—*six* shows in a single year, twice as many as we'd ever done before. It was audacious to think that we could achieve such scale, but I was convinced we had the talent, the funding, and the positive spirit to pull it off. Artists like nothing more than creating and performing, so we were giddy with excitement at the opportunity to really stretch our wings.

One show was small, the seasonal *'Twas the Night Before . . .* , to celebrate Christmas in Chicago and New York. Another was a reboot of our beloved big-top show *Alegria* that had toured for twenty years starting in 1994. We also produced two arena shows—the ice show *Axel* and *Messi10*, a brilliant tribute to the Argentine soccer superstar Lionel Messi that opened to glowing reviews in Barcelona in October. Finally, we planned two resident productions—the action thriller *R.U.N.* at the Luxor resort in Las Vegas and our first permanent show in China, *The Land of Fantasy*, in Hangzhou in August.

The Hangzhou show was the one that had me the most excited—and nervous. It was partly a test of whether we had learned the lesson of *Zaia*, our ill-fated 2008 production on the Chinese island of Macao. As with that show, we were betting that Chinese audiences, steeped in their own circus traditions, would eventually come to accept Cirque's modern aesthetic. While ticket sales for *Zaia* were poor, we were convinced that was because the Chinese visitors to Macao's casinos were interested only in gambling, not entertainment. But just in case, we mitigated our risk in Hangzhou the same way we did in Macao: our partners would not only construct the theater, but also pay for production and operating costs. Our Chinese colleagues were willing to cover these enormous expenses (more than $200 million in all) because their mixed-use real-estate development, the Xintiandi Central Activity Zone, could not get government approval without the type of sophisticated cultural events we provided—yet another demonstration of the power of an elite brand.

As we saw in chapter 4, *Zaia* was driven more by business logic than creative aspiration. We were determined not to make the same mistake with *The Land of Fantasy*. The newly constructed Hangzhou theater was a brilliant work of art all by itself, on the scale of *KÀ* in its technical complexity. It had two sets of revolving bleachers that placed the audience in the center of the story and offered two separate 360-degree views. The stage, meanwhile, was divided into panels that shape shifted into nearly any configuration we could imagine. With 3D props, video mapping, and trapdoors—acrobats seemed to disappear into landscapes and return when you least expected it—*The Land of Fantasy* ranked among our most innovative and technologically advanced productions.

Though Cirque had already toured successfully in China, we knew it would take time for a permanent show to gain traction. But the upsides were strong. Our Hangzhou show could make a powerful statement that we could thrive in China, just as our big Vegas shows proved we could succeed in the United States. That would be a huge breakthrough for Cirque, given the growing affluence of the world's most populous country: China's middle class, estimated at more than 400 million, is larger than the entire population of the United States and is projected to more than double over the next decade. That's why we felt *The Land of Fantasy* could be an inflection point even bigger than *O* was in opening up the substantial market of Las Vegas.

As exciting as it was to see how learning from past mistakes had powered our winning streak into the late 2010s, our latest effort in Vegas, *R.U.N.*, revealed that we are still human after all.

It had been six years since we opened a new resident show on the strip (*Michael Jackson ONE*), and the pressure was intense to come up with something truly original. Not only did we have to offer something substantially different than anything else being offered in Las Vegas, but we had to prove that Cirque was not content to rest on its laurels. Our seventh show in Vegas also had to appeal to both devoted Cirque fans and millennials, our audience of the future.

To accomplish all that, we decided on a mandate that was unusual for us: a live-action thriller using daredevil stunts inspired by Hollywood movies and graphic novels. We hired as director Michael Schwandt, whose credits included TV's *American Idol* and concert tours by Katy Perry and John Legend. After spending nearly a year of mapping out the action sequences— motorcycle stunt riders, martial artists, and pyrotechnics—our creative team found that it kept coming back to the neo-noir crime film *Sin City* for inspiration. So we went directly to the source and hired *Sin City*'s codirector and cowriter Robert Rodriguez to craft a story that would be set in the seedy underside of Las Vegas.

It all sounded great in theory, but by the time *R.U.N.* premiered in October of 2019, we knew we were in trouble. Young audience members loved the show, but our regular fans hated it. The biggest problem: our creative team got so carried away with the story—about a gang war and a protagonist who crashes a wedding—that they forgot people don't come to a Cirque production for narrative and character development. Our fans really only want three things—acrobatics, acrobatics, and more acrobatics—and feel betrayed when they don't get it. *R.U.N.* also did not provide the emotional uplift our audiences expect. It was so dark—especially a gruesome torture scene—that some frustrated customers walked out during the show.

ACCEPT FAILURE

How could we have let *R.U.N.* go so far off the rails? Sometimes your greatest strength—in this case, the creative freedom we give our artists—can also be your biggest weakness. We established our usual checkpoints to monitor the show's development, but our commitment to let our creators freely pursue their vision resulted in some dark digressions that led to failure. In retrospect, we should have intervened and pushed the show in a new direction—or simply taken the Cirque du Soleil name off the production so ticket buyers would not expect something that this particular show could not give them.

It's rare that our drive to innovate backfires so dramatically, but that's a trap any creative company can fall into. The artistic process rarely follows an orderly, direct progression from A to B. There are false starts, dead ends, mistakes, diversions, and missed chances along any road to achievement. In this case, it was hard to distinguish between normal growing pains and a disaster in the making. Either way, it's important to be vigilant about the monitoring process, as we saw with *Varekai* in chapter 2. With *R.U.N.*, that's something we failed to do at considerable cost.

By late February of 2020, four months after opening, we felt we had no choice but to announce that *R.U.N.* would be closing in a matter of days. Pulling the plug on a production is never easy, but we felt we had no choice: the negative reaction on social media and elsewhere was starting to hurt our brand. Sometimes it's better to just throw in the towel than try to overhaul a struggling new venture—which in this case would have been hugely expensive and time-consuming. It was difficult to lose the $20 million we had invested and upsetting to see our close partner MGM Resorts International lose an equal amount. But we tried to mitigate the damage by searching for an outside show to replace *R.U.N.* and bring the crowds the Luxor relies upon, with Cirque serving as producer. We have had an incredibly successful partnership with MGM over the years, and keeping that relationship strong is always a high priority for us.

For any innovative company, failure can often be harder for the business side to accept than it is for the creative team. Artists learn to live daily with mistakes and disappointment as an inevitable part of the process. Shareholders and company executives, on the other hand, can become deeply rattled by a financial loss, vowing to never let it happen again. Leaving the creative side alone is easy when everything is going well, but failure has a way of chipping away at even the most sincere commitments to artistic freedom. Before you know it, the suits are demanding to sit in on planning sessions and offering their opinions. That's when the magic disappears.

Fortunately, that did not happen in this case. But the episode did make TPG realize that after years of substantial investments—$550 million on new shows and acquisitions since 2015—it was time to slow down and shift to a new strategy of optimizing profitability. With a record forty-four productions around the world, it was time to develop new productions at a more sustainable pace and spend the next two or three years recouping our losses from *R.U.N.* and reaping the rewards of TPG's large investments and faith in our brand.

By early 2020, we had much to look forward to. *The Land of Fantasy* was gaining traction: reviews were glowing, and crowds in Hangzhou reached 70 percent of capacity on weekends, a big number for a new market. We had some exciting new shows coming up in the spring—a resident production at Walt Disney World in Orlando and a touring show launching in Montreal. TPG, after steering us through five years of robust growth, was considering taking Cirque public, a huge step that could further raise our profile and feed our continued expansion around the globe.

On a personal note, I was approaching my sixty-seventh birthday in July of 2020. With Cirque on solid footing, having grown by leaps and bounds since my arrival two decades earlier, I thought it was a good time to plan my retirement as CEO—a day I looked forward to with a bittersweet mix of pride, nostalgia, and satisfaction.

That now seems so long ago. We had no idea what was about to hit us.

CHAPTER 7

THE INCREDIBLE POWER
OF A CREATIVE BRAND

Our first hint that 2020 would not be an ordinary year came the way it did for many—with news, in early January, of a deadly virus in Wuhan.

My first concern was for the health and safety of our eighty cast and crew members in our new resident show in China, *The Land of Fantasy*. Fortunately, Hangzhou was not near the epicenter—our show was an eight-hour drive due east from Wuhan—and none of our people had contracted this strange and deadly new infectious disease that health experts were calling COVID-19.

Our relief did not last long. The coronavirus was spreading so rapidly that, on January 23, the Chinese government imposed a nationwide ban on all indoor events of more than one hundred people. That meant closing *The Land of Fantasy* immediately. Next, we had to quickly decide how to best protect our employees, who were getting increasingly worried as each passing day brought more grim news.

TAKE CARE OF YOUR PEOPLE

Technically, our cast and crew were employed by our Chinese partner, the Hangzhou Xintiandi Group (XTD), but that did not influence my thinking. These were *our* people, and it was my responsibility to take care of them. With outbound flights from China being canceled daily, there was not much time to figure out what to do.

My decision was not as simple as one might think. With relatively few cases in Hangzhou, it was not clear whether our people were safer staying indoors or trying to get away on an airplane packed with passengers who might be infected. It reminded me of our crisis nine years earlier in Japan, after a tsunami destroyed the Fukushima nuclear reactor when we had three hundred employees in Tokyo. In both cases, it was difficult to assess the risk at the beginning, but I was guided by the same principle: take care of your employees first, and worry about the cost and implications later. Even in the best of times, creativity will not fully thrive at any company unless its people feel safe and cared for.

As the virus spread, we realized that time was not on our side. Within weeks, I made the call to get everybody out of Hangzhou as soon as possible, before all departing flights were canceled. When the last of our expatriates boarded their planes and made it safely home, I could finally relax and move on to the next challenge.

ROLL WITH THE PUNCHES

On January 30, we had another major decision to make. The epidemic was still in its early stages, but the virus had already made the jump to the island of Hong Kong, where our big-top touring show *Amaluna* was scheduled to open in early April. With the government there closing museums, libraries, and sports events, we decided it would be prudent to cancel our show, too, as a precautionary measure.

Even with two shows canceled, we were not overly worried. COVID-19 appeared to be primarily an Asian phenomenon that we assumed would soon be brought under control. In hindsight, I am amazed at how long it took us—along with the rest of the world—to realize the full extent of the crisis. February has been called "the lost month" as many nations failed to react quickly enough to stem outbreaks that by the end of January had already reached Canada, the United States, Europe, Australia, and Russia.

At Cirque, we were as much in the dark as anyone. Like our counterparts in the worlds of sports, theater, nightclubs, and concerts, we continued to run our business with the conviction that the trillion-dollar live-entertainment industry would always be with us. Businesspeople tend to be optimistic by nature, and as destructive as previous infectious diseases have been—SARS, Ebola, H_1N_1—we never imagined that this new virus would have the power to bring the entire planet to a halt.

By the end of February, the pace of events accelerated rapidly. Nevada had yet to record its first case of COVID-19, but already-nervous organizations were canceling their annual conventions in Las Vegas, causing our advance ticket sales to plummet. Italy was seeing clusters of cases that threatened our upcoming touring dates for *Totem*. Still reeling from the Hangzhou and Hong Kong shutdowns—and reading everything I could about the virus and how it's transmitted—I flew to Vegas on a Thursday for the unpleasant task of closing *R.U.N.*, then hopped on a red-eye flight back to Montreal. Alas, there was no respite back home: creative problems with our next touring show, *Under the Same Sky*, required us to bring in a new director as we geared up for the Montreal premiere in April.

On February 29, as I boarded a flight to Orlando, I was exhausted but consoled myself by remembering that our company had been through difficult periods before. Each time, we emerged better than ever, so I was confident we would get through this crisis too. When your underlying business is strong, the wisest approach is to hang in there and roll with the punches until you can regain your footing. During normal times, that's usually enough.

STAY ON THE CUTTING EDGE

When my flight landed, I headed for Walt Disney World to check in on rehearsals for our new resident production, a collaboration with Disney called *Drawn to Life*. Finally, some good news: the show was spectacular, shaping up to become one of our best ever.

A great deal was riding on this project. Before retiring, I wanted to make sure that Cirque came out with one more unforgettable show. To keep our brand synonymous with cutting-edge creativity, I had always felt we needed at least one groundbreaking production every few years. Our touring shows had all been amazingly successful—in fact, in nearly four decades, we've never had a miss—but our biggest artistic statements seemed to come from elaborate resident productions like *O*, *KÀ*, and *The Beatles LOVE*. In 2020, the show with the most potential to become that breakthrough event was *Drawn to Life*.

The concept for this production was hatched when our previous show at Walt Disney World, *La Nouba*, ended in 2017 after a remarkable nineteen-year run. Not wanting to lose the magnificent 1,700-seat theater to another production, I was excited when Disney offered to collaborate with us on a new show using its iconic intellectual property. At first, the idea did not go over well at our Montreal headquarters, as some employees had reservations about how well Disney characters would fit into a Cirque show. But after teaming up successfully with singular creative forces such as the Beatles and Michael Jackson, I saw this as yet another opportunity to produce something truly original and spectacular.

At rehearsals that day, it was thrilling to watch the show coming together so well. Under director Michel Laprise, who had already scored hits with *Kurios* and *Séptimo Día—No Descansaré*, we decided to focus on the parallels between hand-drawn animation and human performance. The similarities are remarkable: watching an acrobat performing a stunt in slow-motion replay is very similar to the incremental movement of a hand-drawn cartoon figure coming to life as sketchbook pages are flipped. In creating this production, we wanted to use the latest stage technology to seamlessly blend these two disciplines. At the rehearsal, I watched in amazement as the interplay between acrobats and animated figures gave life to a moving story of a girl who discovers unfinished drawings by her late father and embarks on a dramatic journey featuring Disney characters from her childhood.

When the rehearsal was over, I stood and cheered, feeling reinvigorated. It reminded me of what I love so much about my job: the chance to work with supremely creative people and help launch these miraculous shows. I had no doubt that *Drawn to Life* would be the breakthrough we were all so eager for. Afterward, as I greeted the cast and crew with hugs, handshakes, and smiles, we were all blissfully unaware of the heartbreak to follow.

KEEP COOL UNDER PRESSURE

By the beginning of March, COVID-19 had spread to all regions of Italy, where hospitals had become dangerously overcrowded.

With *Totem* scheduled to open in Rome on April 1—and the big-top tent already set up—our local promoter decided to shut it down after health authorities warned of "widespread ongoing transmission." The show was scheduled to travel to Milan in May, but that was canceled as well. Within days, Italy went into a nationwide lockdown.

Meanwhile, our Blue Man Group world tour had been planning an April 14 opening in Seoul, South Korea, but infections were running so high there we had to cancel that production too. We scrambled to reroute our canceled shows in Hong Kong, Italy, and South Korea to other parts of the world not affected by the virus—until it became clear that such areas did not exist. Soon, the World Health Organization would declare a global pandemic.

Starting March 9, our shows began falling like dominoes: *Corteo*'s tour of Antwerp, Vienna, and Montpellier were shut down, as were *Kooza* in Lyon and *Luzia* in the Canary Islands. The following day, *Kooza*'s Tel Aviv tour in June was shuttered. *Volta* and *Axel* in California and the Blue Man Group in Cairo were canceled on March 11—the same day the NBA shocked the sports world by abruptly suspending its season when one of its players tested positive for COVID-19.

After nearly twenty years of dealing with the endless stream of crises that come with running a global live-entertainment company—not to mention my previous career in crisis-management public relations—I thought I knew something about handling an emergency. But nothing could have prepared me for this. At Cirque headquarters, people were constantly bursting into my office to deliver yet more bad news. At hastily arranged executive meetings, every decision we made was outdated by the time the meeting was over—another city had locked down, another show was canceled, another border was closed—so we had to immediately call another meeting. Each gathering began the same way, with someone saying, "It's getting worse." Normally, I would fly anywhere in the world to help troubleshoot problems that had cropped up, but that had become impossible. The risks of contracting the disease on a flight or getting stuck in some faraway city were too great.

On March 12, the bottom fell out completely. Seventy-one performances were canceled in a single day, comprising nearly every scheduled show of Cirque's thirteen touring productions in North America, Europe, Asia, Australia, and the Middle East between March and October, plus the rest of the Blue Man Group world tour. Within days, we also shut down the last few remaining dates of our touring shows and three resident productions (*Joyà* in Mexico, *Paramour* in Hamburg, and—most painfully—the gestating *Drawn to Life* at Walt Disney World) plus another twenty shows under our subsidiaries Blue Man Group, VStar, and The Works.

On Friday, March 13, our board of directors had a conference call to discuss what the hell to do. At least our six Las Vegas resident shows were still running. Maybe we could hang on to those to keep some revenue coming in. They couldn't shut down the entire multibillion-dollar entertainment industry of Las Vegas, could they?

Yes, they could. The next day, I was at my hair salon when my cell phone rang. No sooner had I finished that conversation than it rang again. And again. And again. The interruptions were driving my poor stylist crazy. With each call, I tried to absorb the new mind-bending reality: Nevada was shutting down all nonessential businesses. The big casino resorts, where our remaining six shows were in residence, were closing indefinitely.

We were, in a word, toast. In less than one week, we went from forty-four productions worldwide and over $1 billion in annual sales to zero shows and no revenue. On Sunday, our board held another emergency conference call, but there was not much to say. The two components our company is based upon—the ability to transport people and equipment around the world to produce live shows and then assemble large audiences to watch them—had suddenly disappeared. We were left, quite literally, without a business.

What to do? I had no idea. All I knew was that I had to stay calm. When times get tough, I become what I would call a "cool fighter." I say "cool" because I rarely lose my temper. The more pressure there is, the more focused I get. I'm fortunate in that respect. Throwing chairs might feel good for a moment, but it's impossible to think clearly when you're out of control. In times of crisis, it's so important to take a deep breath, figure out what your top priorities are, and create a plan of action.

And I say "fighter" because I never give up. I am not an aggressive person, but I am tenacious. I never lose track of the final goal, whether it's the seemingly endless negotiations with the Beatles or getting our company back on track after the Great Recession. I know I'm not a particularly charismatic leader. My actions are far more compelling than my words. Especially at this point, with the very survival of our company at stake, there was no time for grandstanding or wallowing in self-pity.

There was, however, lots of work to do. My first priority was to take care of our employees stranded abroad. Canceling all those shows had suddenly sent our fifteen hundred cast and crew members adrift, scattered across thirteen cities around the world. They all had to be immediately sent back to their home countries—thirty nations in all—as the virus wreaked havoc on the world's transportation systems.

This was a Herculean job for our staff, made more difficult because most of our Montreal employees were working from home now, thanks to the virus. In all, thirty people worked full-time on the repatriation project. It was exceedingly complex. We had to route some employees through two or three cities to get them home. It also wasn't cheap. The cost of flights, hotels, and meals ran into the millions, but we never stopped to consider the expense. Our main enemy was time. We had to rush people home before their national borders slammed shut.

Somehow, we finished just in time, allowing us to move on to the next logistical hurdle: finding warehouses to store the massive amount of equipment each touring production requires—up to fifty giant containers per show. In all, 483 trucks were loaded up with literally tons of lighting and sound equipment, aerial rigging, big-top tents, employee food service, concession stands, and more.

At long last, it was over. All our shows were fully closed up—twenty-three Cirque productions and twenty-one by our affiliated brands—and all our employees were safely back home, our touring equipment securely tucked away.

Next came the biggest challenge of all: keeping alive a company that had no revenue and would have to wait months, perhaps years, to start up again. Of all the astonishing feats Cirque du Soleil had attempted during its thirty-six years of existence, this was by far the most daunting.

SHORT-TERM PAIN FOR LONG-TERM GAIN

In the middle of March 2020, the novel coronavirus was not well understood. But one thing was clear: it wasn't going away anytime soon. Experts were predicting a minimum of twelve to eighteen months before a vaccine could be developed—possibly much longer—and live entertainment would be among the last industries to come back. Along with theaters, nightclubs, and concert venues, it would be hard to think of a company more decimated by this grim new reality than Cirque du Soleil.

Though I was determined to save our company, I was not the owner, which meant that the most important decisions were out of my hands. I began taking part in conference calls attended by more than forty players, including investment bankers specializing in corporate restructuring and teams of lawyers, business advisers, and accountants. With no revenue coming in, our advisers said, we simply did not have the funds to pay the $400 million annual expense for salaries. Whatever cash we had, or could raise quickly from the owners, would have to go to keeping the company functioning at a basic level so we could go through the complex and lengthy corporate restructuring process made necessary by the crisis—keeping Cirque alive, in other words, until our shows could go back up. The alternative was to fold up our circus tents and shut down our Montreal headquarters for good, negating the need for any employees at all. But we were not about to do that. The only way to get to the other side of this pandemic was as clear as it was heartbreaking: we would have to lay off the vast majority of our workforce.

March 19 was, without doubt, one of the worst days of my life. That's when I had to announce the immediate reduction of 95 percent of our staff, everyone from performing artists to senior executives. A total of 4,679 people lost their jobs that day. We fully expected to rehire them all when our shows went back up, but we had no idea when that might be.

I knew we had no choice—sometimes, you must endure short-term pain for long-term gain—but thinking about how our beloved creators, technicians, and support staff would survive was exceedingly painful. The irony was hard to miss: to save the company, I had to violate the very purpose of my life—creating jobs for artists. Throughout this book, I have talked about the importance of taking care of your employees, how critical they are to the creative output of any company, and how hard managers must work to make them feel safe and secure. All of that remains true. But now the ax was falling, and I was the one swinging it.

We did whatever we could to mitigate the suffering, including paying unused vacation time and maintaining health insurance coverage, at least for the time being. I cut my own pay by 50 percent. We retained a core support team of 175 employees in Montreal and Las Vegas to perform essential functions like information technology, planning future tours and ticket sales, and preparing for the eventual rehiring process. The whole ordeal was excruciating, by far the most difficult days in Cirque's history.

Normally, I would make an announcement like this to employees in person, but social distancing had emptied our headquarters and all cast members and crews were back home. So I had to break the news by video, delivered on a special network. It was a surreal scene, sitting at my desk (alone except for a video technician), staring into the camera to make the announcement. During normal times, our headquarters would be bursting with activity: the chatter of dozens of languages, athletes in tracksuits striding through the halls excitedly discussing their work, designers rummaging through fabric in the costume department. Now it was mostly empty. Our rehearsal studios, usually full of acrobats flying through the air as they rehearsed a new show, were deserted. "This is tough, I know," I heard myself say into the camera, "but we will fight the fight together."

Through it all, I kept my emotions at bay. Most days, I was running on adrenaline as I met with staff, connected with our board of directors, and fielded calls from reporters. Normally, I am not afraid of showing emotion during a tragedy, like when I met with cast and crew in Tampa after the fatal accident at one of our shows. Even happy times, like a magical premiere, can bring tears to my eyes. But not now. There was too much to do. To win this fight, I had to stay focused.

A few weeks later, the gravity of the moment finally overcame me. One night, after a long day of media interviews, I couldn't sleep. At 3:30 a.m., I checked my iPad to see what was being published. One story in particular made my blood rise. I was quoted accurately, but the headline suggested that Cirque's level of debt was the culprit, not the pandemic. Angry at the misleading spin, it took me a long time to get back to sleep. In the morning, I went to our mostly deserted headquarters to work out in our gym, hoping that would relieve the stress. When I arrived, a man and woman from the costume department were coming in to pick up their belongings. "Monsieur Lamarre, keep fighting for us," the woman said, choking up. "We *need* you." I had to fight back tears too. When they left, my sour mood evaporated and my motivation came surging back. I was more determined than ever to fight to give our people their jobs back.

VALUE CREATIVITY ABOVE ALL

The media coverage in Quebec tended to focus on the most sensational aspect of our story: the large debt on our balance sheets. There was no disagreement about the facts: the TPG group owed $900 million, money it had borrowed to finance the purchase of the company in 2015 and the string of acquisitions that followed.

Such leveraged buyouts are common in the private-equity business, allowing the buyer to mitigate risk—and, in our case, helping the acquired company to grow, creating jobs. Our lenders, meanwhile, considered these loans a smart investment because we were an extremely successful, trusted company with $1 billion in annual revenue and a healthy debt-to-profit (EBITDA) ratio of four to one.

After five years of investing its own money and borrowed capital into Cirque, the TPG group entered 2020 ready to finally reap what it had sown. The plan was to lower expenses by easing up on new-show development, continue paying off debt, optimize profit, and prepare an exit by filing for an IPO or selling the company outright. Using the typical private-equity ownership time frame of five to seven years, the strategy made perfect sense—until, that is, a once-in-a-lifetime pandemic struck.

When we laid off our employees, we were criticized for being so highly leveraged. But when our revenue dropped to zero, it didn't matter how much we owed. Whether it was $900 million or $300 million or fifty cents, we still could not pay our bills. Nor could we pay the interest on our loans, so we defaulted for the first time ever. An unforeseen health crisis that crippled the entire planet is what rendered us unable to pay employees, freelancers, suppliers, and creditors, not our debt.

It was during these bleak moments, when Cirque du Soleil was flat on its back, that I came to a startling realization that instantly lifted my mood: not only could we survive this pandemic, but we could thrive again. I knew this because we began fielding dozens of calls from investors all over the world inquiring about buying us. As devastated as we were, our brand was so strong, and our intellectual property so valuable, that we were still considered a highly desirable acquisition.

Those excited phone calls perfectly dramatize the incredible power of creativity in the world of business. Because what, really, does Cirque du Soleil own? We have no physical products (aside from some merchandising). No factories. No valuable inventory or expensive real estate. We do, however, have a secret ingredient worth more than any of those things combined, a special sauce that made us a hugely attractive investment even in the worst of times: the creativity of our artists. Harnessing that magic has produced an immensely valuable asset, our intellectual property, and a beloved brand name instantly recognized the world over. *That's* what potential buyers wanted to buy—even when we had zero revenue—because they knew it was a great investment. And that's why, even from a strictly Darwinian point of view, the best strategy for any business is to prioritize creativity.

Once I realized Cirque was not only viable, but still highly desirable, I got out of bed inspired every morning and drove to our nearly empty headquarters repeating my mantra, *I will bring our employees back*. That's what fed me.

IGNORE THE NOISE

Fortunately, I was hardly alone in this fight; I had my stellar team beside me every step of the way. From the moment we shut down in March, my seven-day-a-week routine was to arrive at our nearly deserted headquarters at 7:00 a.m., work out in the gym, and meet with Jocelyn Côté, our general counsel, and Stéphane Lefebvre, our chief financial officer (later promoted to chief operating officer and eventually chief executive officer). Virtually at first, and later in our offices with masks and social distancing, the three of us would report on the latest developments and establish our most urgent priorities. Later in the day, our circle would include Lyne Lamothe, chief talent officer, who handled our employees; two executives who oversee our shows—Diane Quinn, chief creative officer, and Eric Grilly, executive vice president (who called in from Las Vegas by Zoom)—and Caroline Couillard, now our global head of public relations. Those six advisers, confidantes, and good friends were alongside me in the trenches every day as we battled the pandemic together.

Though our main goal was to keep the company afloat until we could bring our shows back—whenever that might be—I also felt a deep responsibility to help our laid-off workers financially and settle with our freelance artists who had not been paid for work performed. The question was, how? We had zero revenue, little cash on hand, and a burn rate of $6 million per month (to pay salaries, to fund medical insurance for six hundred laid-off Las Vegas employees, and to just keep the lights on).

Clearly, to have any hope of surviving, Cirque would have to file for bankruptcy protection and restructure the company in a way that satisfied our creditors. The TPG group wanted to retain control, but it would have to bid like everybody else. Any court-approved deal would require not only the settlement of our $900 million debt, but an infusion of several hundred million dollars to keep us functioning until the pandemic was over. While we were excited to see investors from all over the world inquiring about submitting bids, that created another problem: Quebec's political and business leaders became worried that a foreign buyer might move our operations outside of Canada.

For many, that was unthinkable. Imagine what the Yankees mean to New York City and you have a good idea of how we are regarded in Quebec. In Montreal, residents like to say we are known for two things—the Canadiens hockey team and Cirque du Soleil. The economic impact alone of losing Cirque would be immense. In an average year, our touring shows in Canada generate up to $120 million of economic activity. Our work with nearly three thousand suppliers contributes another $277 million to the national economy. And that's not even counting the potential loss of thousands of jobs at Cirque and other companies across the country that we affect, the millions in taxes we pay, and our significant donations to charity.

To stave off that disaster, the government of Quebec offered Cirque a $200 million loan through its investment arm, Investissement Québec, on the condition that our headquarters and senior executives remain in the province. The TPG group agreed and on June 29 made a formal bid to keep control by having Cirque file for bankruptcy protection. Our owners would invest $100 million of their own money, which, together with the $200 million loan from Quebec, would give TPG and its partners a 55 percent ownership share. The lenders would receive a 45 percent stake, which worked out to about forty cents on the dollar for its $900 million in loans.

Whether Cirque's creditors or the court would accept this deal remained to be seen, but my eye was on the long game. Regardless of who ended up owning Cirque, I wanted to make sure our artists got paid. Fortunately, I was able to convince the TPG group to establish, as part of its proposal, a $20 million fund for our artists and employees—$15 million for laid-off workers and $5 million to pay our freelancers. That fund would probably never have materialized without Quebec's timely loan offer, which kept the TPG group in the game and allowed me to lobby hard for the money.

As a result, the day we filed for bankruptcy protection was bittersweet. On one hand, it was clearly a sad moment, an all-time low in the history of our company. On the other hand, being protected from our creditors meant that Cirque had an excellent chance of surviving—and the inclusion of the $20 million workers' fund instantly put tremendous pressure on other potential investors to offer the same terms.

As my team and I worked with a dizzying array of bankers, lawyers, accountants, and advisers to rescue Cirque, there were many moments when it was difficult to focus because of all the outside noise. Media pundits, politicians, former employees, anonymous sources, and others freely took shots at us. "Cirque has been badly mismanaged," they said. "The executive leadership" (i.e., me) "has to go." "The company's time has passed." "Cirque is being propped up by an insider's handout from Quebec ministers at taxpayers' expense" (never mind that it was a loan, not a grant). And more. Painting ownership, management, and our supporters as villains seemed to satisfy some critics, but their arguments missed the most important point: we were living through a once-in-a-century pandemic that had shut down the whole live-entertainment industry worldwide. Before that, we were thriving.

People at creative companies will recognize the unspoken assumption that often underlies such criticism: *There's something flaky and irresponsible about highly innovative firms. Those artsy types don't really know how to run a business.* Sometimes other culprits are blamed: *Those cutthroat financial people in charge have betrayed the creative roots of the company.* When such media narratives take hold, they can be hard to dispel.

One of our toughest moments came on June 12. What should have been a joyous day—the thirty-sixth anniversary of Cirque du Soleil's founding—was instead a painful one. A group of freelancers gathered at the site of our big-top tent performances in Montreal's Old Port to protest against management and demand

$1.5 million in back pay owed to 115 artists. Yes, we owed that money, and it was terribly upsetting that we could not pay them just yet. But because I could not discuss the issue publicly (for legal reasons), it was not widely known that I had been working furiously behind the scenes to get those artists paid.

At such moments, it's tempting to fight back, launch a counter PR campaign, and leak information to clear your good name. In this case, I wished the general public had a few facts: the pandemic had sent thousands of well-managed Quebec companies out of business forever, while we were very much alive and coming back through the long restructuring process. But trying to micromanage the media is a losing battle. There are only so many hours in a day. Better to ignore the noise and focus your precious time and energy doing your job—in this case, saving our company and making sure our artists got paid—and have faith that the truth will eventually come out.

It also helps to keep some perspective. Most of the negative stories were of keen interest to the Quebec media but did not travel far. People in Las Vegas, Orlando, Europe, Asia, and beyond didn't seem to care much about our local controversies. International media outlets tended to focus on the real bottom line: that after being decimated by the virus, Cirque was making great progress in its fight to come back.

VISUALIZE SUCCESS

The terms of Cirque's bankruptcy protection filing, it turned out, were not well received by our creditors. They let the court know, in no uncertain terms, that the $900 million they were owed should be worth far more than a mere 45 percent of the company.

And the judge listened. In such cases, the lenders' views carry considerable weight.

Two weeks before the filing, my executive team and I had our first direct contact with our creditors. Expecting the worst—bankers who are owed vast sums can be antagonistic, to say the least—we were pleasantly surprised to find them charming and solicitous. "Guys, you shouldn't be afraid of us," they said. "We want to be your partner. Our goal is to own the company and leave your existing management team in place. We believe in your brand and see great success ahead."

Those words seemed too good to be true, so we were naturally suspicious at first. Were they just saying that to drive up the price of the company—and the value of their defaulted loans—when it came time for other investors to make bids?

Over the ensuing weeks and months, we were delighted to find, our lenders never wavered from their position. They had consulted with the owners of our Las Vegas venues, MGM Resorts International, who strongly recommended that they offer to retain me and my executive team. "Daniel and his crew know what they're doing," MGM's executives said. "That's why they've had so much success for the past twenty years." Our creditors never deviated from their pledge to keep our headquarters in Montreal, did not need the $200 million loan from Quebec, and promised to invest $375 million of their own funds to get Cirque back up and running.

Crucially, I was ecstatic to hear, our lenders would follow TPG's lead and offer a $20 million fund for artists and laid-off employees. Their $375 million bid, together with the $900 million they were owed, established a $1.275 billion valuation for our company—an astonishing number considering that a vaccine had still not been developed and we had no prospects of revenue anytime soon (remarkably, that valuation was only slightly below the $1.5 billion the company sold for in 2015). Any other bidders hoping to own Cirque would have to top that figure.

The TPG group, unable to match that offer, eventually dropped out. It was sad, some months later, when I attended our last board meeting with our former owners. These executives from TPG Capital (especially Jim Coulter, David Bonderman, and David Trujillo), Fosun International, and Caisse de dépôt et placement du Québec had become good friends and respected partners. Together, the group had lost hundreds of millions of dollars in a matter of months. I was also sad to part ways with our chairman, Mitch Garber, a great Canadian businessman who had done so much for Cirque over the years. At that final Zoom meeting, I think we were all feeling a bit stunned that such an extraordinary collection of business minds had been defeated by a microscopic virus.

More than a dozen other investors—who had clearly hoped to scoop Cirque up at fire-sale prices—also dropped out when they saw the size of our lenders' bid. In the end, Cirque made presentations to just five remaining potential suitors—including my old friend Guy Laliberté, who had teamed up with an investment group in hopes of returning to the company he had founded decades ago. (In February of 2020, Guy had sold his final 10 percent ownership stake to Caisse de dépôt et placement du Québec.) None of them, however, were willing to match the $1.275 billion offered by our creditors.

In September, the court announced that our lenders had won the auction, allowing the deal-closing process to begin. That's when I knew that the company had been saved. Far from being adversaries, our creditors had become trusted partners committed to investing significant resources to ensure our survival.

During the summer and fall, I got to know our likely new owners much better. Since there were four major players, we started calling them the Fab Four. Forty investment firms would own a slice of Cirque du Soleil, once the deal was completed, but these four would have a controlling interest of about 53 percent: Gabriel de Alba of the Catalyst Capital Group, based in Toronto; Charles "Chip" Rini of CBAM Partners of New York (part of a larger firm, Eldridge Industries, that owns a stake in the Los Angeles Dodgers); Stephen Ketchum, founder of Sound Point Capital Management of New York; and Joe Rodbard of Benefit Street Partners of New York.

What impressed me most about our prospective new owners was their eagerness to learn about our unusual business—and their patience. They understood that it could be a long time before the live-entertainment industry returned to anything approximating normal. Rushing back too soon could not only cost them millions but also seriously damage the brand. "We desperately want the shows to go back up," they told us, "but only when conditions are right."

By then, there were already glimmers of hope. After its early missteps, the government of China had COVID-19 under control enough to allow *The Land of Fantasy* to reopen in Hangzhou on May 26, 2020. Because of travel restrictions, our artists still could not reenter the country and had to be replaced with Chinese performers (who followed strict safety protocols), but the mask-wearing, socially distant crowds enjoyed the production, and ticket sales were encouraging. We were also excited to see our *Joyà* dinner-theater show start up again in Mexico on July 3, 2020, though it had to be shut down temporarily in the fall due to an outbreak. Like professional sports teams that experienced interruptions in their schedules, we only returned when it was safe. These reopenings also gave us valuable experience as we prepared for the eventual restaging of our other shows.

Through all the drama of our ownership battles and tentative steps toward reopening, I learned an important lesson about surviving tough times. When faced with a crisis of this magnitude, it's important to not just *hope* for success, but to actively visualize it.

All difficult tasks—and, let's face it, all acts of creation are exceedingly difficult—come with moments of worry and doubt. That negative energy makes it very hard to visualize success, never mind accomplish it. So the first step is to clear your mind by letting those anxieties go. Don't share them with your team because that can make everyone around you insecure and fearful. "If Daniel's worried," they'll say, "then we're *really* in trouble."

Instead, look for encouragement wherever you can find it. For me, an unexpected source of inspiration came from my daily exchanges with building employees—our janitors, security guards, and others—as I walked through our nearly deserted headquarters.

"Hey, you're not giving up, are you?" they'd say.

"No way!" I'd shout. "We're on our way back!"

During upsetting times, I was surprised to find, these small exchanges gave me the courage to face another day with the positive energy I needed everyone around me to feel. And that optimistic frame of mind helped with the next step: actually visualizing the outcomes I was striving for. I began imagining myself arriving at the first postpandemic showing of *O* at the Bellagio in Las Vegas, feeling the excitement of the buzzing crowd. Sitting in the audience for the premiere of *Drawn to Life*, our fabulous new production with Disney. Watching employees flooding back into our headquarters chatting excitedly about their various projects.

This process is much like the rituals our athletes and artists perform as they prepare to go onstage. In their minds, they will slow down their routines to microseconds and watch themselves perform each miraculous feat flawlessly. So, when the moment comes to do it for real, it has become automatic (there being no time to consciously *think* before doing). It's the same for any creative endeavor, whether carving a sculpture or finding solutions for a complex business deal. Visualizing the process and the desired outcome can make success feel inevitable.

Quite unconsciously, I began another ritual every morning when I walked through our Alley of Clowns corridor. Passing those fantastic photographs, I couldn't help but smile. I started imagining our brilliant clowns breaking free from the prison of their homes to appear back onstage to make people laugh again.

BALANCING ACTS

In November of 2020, eight months after the pandemic shut us down, I was in Jocelyn's office with Stéphane listening to a conference call on speakerphone.

"Are you okay?" a voice said.

"Yes," came the reply.

This pattern repeated itself dozens of times. A lawyer would say, "Are you okay?" or words to that effect. Then, one by one, each of our new owners would answer affirmatively to the terms of the transaction.

With the final "Yes!" the call ended. Cirque du Soleil officially had new owners! The three of us erupted with cheers (only partly muffled by our masks). We wanted to hug and high-five but managed to restrain ourselves. Then we raced into the hallway to gather with Lyne, Diane, Caroline, and about twenty other employees who emerged from other parts of the building to pop open a bottle of champagne. We had won the war!

Later, we announced the closing of the transaction. My old friend Jim Murren, former CEO and chairman of MGM Resorts International, would become cochairman of the board alongside Gabriel de Alba of Catalyst Capital. The response of the worldwide press to the news that Cirque would survive was overwhelming. I spent fourteen hours doing interviews with television networks, websites, newspapers, and magazines, reaching a potential audience of five billion people around the world. As word ricocheted around the internet, we got thousands of emails and millions of social media posts saying things like, "We are so happy that Cirque is back! When are you coming back to my city?" The massive interest proved that our brand, astonishingly, was just as strong as it was the moment we shut down.

Our announcement had another purpose: I wanted to send a message of hope to our current and former employees and let them know that some compensation was on its way. For our thousands of laid-off employees, the $15 million fund worked out to several thousand dollars each as a supplement to their unemployment benefits. And our freelancers would be paid in full from the $5 million fund. These gestures weren't nearly enough, we knew, since our people still had to find ways to survive until our shows went back up. Unable to fix that grim situation, I recommitted myself to things I could control: plotting the next stage of our comeback. That meant relaunching our productions as soon as it was safe to do so.

After spending most of 2020 focused on the financial side of the business, I was relieved to be able to start thinking about the creative side again. Many of the stories in this book involve the delicate balancing act we all perform between the creative and the practical, the dreaming and the bill paying. Like acrobats on a high wire, we must each find that precarious balance that keeps us moving forward without falling. By the time our ownership situation was resolved, Cirque du Soleil had clearly lost that equilibrium. Our company had become defined—internally and in the public eye—by investors, lawyers, and accountants, not by artists, creative directors, and costume designers. The imbalance served as a stark reminder of what really matters. No amount of money or financial expertise could ever replace our raison d'être—the act of dreaming up shows and presenting them to an audience. That dynamic is true for any company. Without a passionate creative core, you have nothing. Especially in a crisis, those intangible sparks of inspiration must never be snuffed out by the demands of the business side—as they were, for us and far too many others, during that awful pandemic year.

CHERISH YOUR PASSIONATE EMPLOYEES

So it was tremendously exciting in December of 2020 when the first COVID-19 vaccine was approved in both Canada and the United States and we could finally start thinking about getting our shows back up. It was immediately apparent that our first priority should be our Las Vegas resident shows because most of those artists were still living in the area. With international borders still largely closed, none of our touring productions could open until our people were permitted to travel—and that could take a while.

As 2021 began—and I celebrated my twentieth anniversary at Cirque, a milestone that just a few months earlier I wasn't sure I would reach!—we had two pressing questions: When would Las Vegas be safe enough to allow large gatherings, and how long would it take to assemble our casts of artists? It goes without saying that our people isolating at home didn't have trapezes hanging in their living rooms. At the same time, we would never risk the health of our artists until they were 100 percent ready to perform.

Fortunately, COVID-19 case counts, hospitalizations, and death rates came down relatively quickly as the United States rolled out its vaccination program. By April, talks with our Las Vegas casino partners and Nevada government officials had made considerable progress. Originally, we had planned for *O* at the Bellagio to be our first show back. It's our signature event and the biggest-selling production in the world (no show has sold as many tickets over the previous two-plus decades). But the owner of Treasure Island Hotel Casino, Phil Ruffin, was passionate about *Mystère* reopening at his venue as soon as possible. (Phil had bought Treasure Island from MGM Mirage in 2009.) There would be a certain poetic justice to having *Mystère* open first; it was our first Vegas resident show when it opened in 1993, and its success forever changed the entertainment landscape of the city.

On April 21, we were able to announce, with great fanfare, that after more than a year of dark theaters, Cirque du Soleil was rising again—"Intermission Is Over!" as we put it. *Mystère* would relaunch on June 28 and *O* on July 1. We even managed to schedule two touring productions—*Kooza* in Punta Cana, Dominican Republic, in November and *Luzia* at London's Royal Albert Hall in January 2022. We also announced that the Blue

Man Group would return to the Luxor Hotel and Casino in Las Vegas in late June.

My video call with employees was quite emotional, as you can imagine, as the news we had dreamed about for so long was finally coming true. On the tiny faces visible on my computer screen, I could see people choking up. When the call ended, my exemplary longtime executive assistant, Rita Fiorante, came into my office, her eyes also filled with tears. I had trouble maintaining my composure too. After the trauma of mass layoffs, I was finally back to doing what I was put on Earth to do: create jobs for artists.

Now came the hard work of reassembling our shows. We only had two months to get our complex productions up and running, and I had no idea what kind of shape our performers were in. Soon enough, I was stunned by reports from our directors in Vegas that nearly all of them were in excellent condition. They had been amazingly resourceful during the pandemic, setting up acrobatic apparatuses in their garages and backyards, working out hard, and keeping tabs on each other to make sure they kept the faith. I knew our artists were a special bunch—a peek at any show makes that obvious—but I hadn't fully appreciated, until that moment, how truly extraordinary they were. It was a powerful validation of our casting process, one that never anticipated our people would have to pass such a surreal test that challenged their commitment as never before.

In the weeks leading up to our reopenings, ticket sales went through the roof. As Las Vegas opened up and tourists flooded the city, there was so much pent-up demand for live entertainment that our daily sales were double the normal volume. We were also inundated with calls from promoters, government agencies, developers, and arts organizations from around the world asking when we could bring our shows to their cities. It was like nothing we had seen in years. Not only was our brand not tarnished or forgotten during the long hiatus; it was more popular than ever.

When I arrived in Las Vegas in late June, the atmosphere was electric. At dress rehearsals, the excitement was palpable in every hug, air-kiss, and high five. We were inundated with press inquiries from around the world, and I spent long days doing interviews that made me realize the profound significance of this moment: with Broadway theaters still dark, Las Vegas and Cirque had become a global symbol of the resurrection of live entertainment.

Finally, it was time for *Mystère* to open. The sold-out crowd was buzzing with anticipation. As always, the show began with a clown holding a strange bird. But this time, after reminding the audience not to smoke or take pictures, he added, "Intermission is over; Cirque du Soleil is back!" The audience roared, and the energy onstage was explosive. Our artists were in peak form, as if there never had been a break at all.

During those dark days in Montreal, stranded in our nearly empty headquarters, I dreamed of this moment often. But I never imagined that the waves of emotion coming from the audience and performers would be *this* powerful. If the pandemic created some of the worst days of my life, the reopening of *Mystère* surely ranked among the best. Such a long journey from nightmare to pure joy.

Three days later, for the reopening of *O*, we staged an elaborate preshow celebration that began with two limousines pulling up to the Bellagio. Bill Hornbuckle, CEO of MGM Resorts International, and I each greeted one of the limos by opening the door. I will never forget our cast members, fully dressed in costume, jumping from the limo into my arms, one by one, and hugging me as cameras clicked from the horde of assembled media. Then we strode into the Bellagio for a parade through the resort as people cheered, handed out flowers, and held up signs saying things like, "Welcome Back!" and "What a Happy Day!"

At showtime, as Emmanuelle and I entered the theater, an usher approached me. "Sir, you don't know me, but I know you," he said. "I haven't worked for fifteen months, and now you are giving me my job back." He hugged me and said, "I just want to thank you."

O was a revelation, flawlessly executed and bursting with emotion. After the show, I met with the cast and crew onstage, behind the curtain. After we passed around glasses of champagne, I introduced them to our management team and our new owner and cochairman of the board, Gabriel de Alba. Then I tried to find the words to thank them.

"So it's impossible to me not to talk with my heart, because that was a long, long adventure," I told them, admitting that there were times when I wasn't sure whether the company would survive. But we came back, I said, because "you guys, the artists, had faith, and how have you shown us your faith? By continuing to train, to stay in shape. And that was so inspiring for us, you know? We were alone in the office just thinking about the first night of our show in Vegas, and now"—here I teared up, the immensity of our accomplishment and deep gratitude hitting me full force—"we are living the dream, and I wanted to thank you because . . ." Still choking, I had a final thought to squeeze out, loudly: ". . . we're back!"

After the group toast, I went around the stage and approached each and every member of the cast and crew, some two hundred people in all, and toasted them individually to say, "Thank you!"

Cherish your passionate employees. Without them, your company cannot survive—during a pandemic or otherwise. With them, you have a limitless reservoir of creativity that can power your organization to new heights. How that plays out differs for each person and each company, of course. For us, it means developing spectacular shows that leave audiences gasping in wonder, inspired to expand their own boundaries, chase their dreams, and believe that anything is possible.

EPILOGUE

FINDING OPPORTUNITY
IN A NEW WORLD

As we relaunched the company in the summer of 2021, it felt a bit like the crazy old days, when we opened one new show after another, running on pure adrenaline. As this book was going to press, we had just rebooted the Blue Man Group, *Mystère*, and *O* in Las Vegas in the same week and were busy rehearsing Cirque's three remaining resident productions there—*The Beatles LOVE* and *Michael Jackson ONE*, scheduled for August, and *KÀ* in the fall. Our new Disney collaboration in Orlando, *Drawn to Life*, would follow by the end of the year.

Meanwhile, I was already meeting with our resort partners to plan the development of new productions. In Mexico, Daniel Chávez Morán gave an enthusiastic go-ahead for the dinner show we had been planning at his beautiful Vidanta Nuevo Vallarta resort, now slated for 2024. In Las Vegas, MGM chief Bill Hornbuckle and his COO, Corey Sanders (who is on our board of directors), asked us to continue creating new content for their properties in Vegas and abroad. That's in addition to a new cabaret show we are developing for MGM to replace *Zumanity* at its New York–New York Hotel & Casino.

We also had our hands full planning to restart dozens of touring shows from Cirque and our affiliate brands Blue Man Group, VStar Entertainment Group (*PAW Patrol*, *Trolls*), and

The Works Entertainment (The Illusionists magic shows). As conditions become safer around the world, especially in Europe and Asia, we plan to be back at full strength in 2023.

FOCUS ON QUALITY

While all of that was very exciting—and we'll still be in the middle of our relaunch by the time this book is published—I vowed not to become addicted to the rush of opening shows. That was a big lesson from earlier periods in our history, when we developed too many new productions at once and the quality suffered.

That's not to say that we are retrenching. Far from it. We are still working hard to restore nearly all of the forty-plus shows that were running when the shutdown occurred. But during the long hiatus, we realized that we had sometimes become too ambitious for our own good. Going forward, we will launch new productions at a more measured pace. One new resident show per year should be our limit, giving us the time to focus on quality and nurture each production carefully; it also ensures we have the resources to fix problems that inevitably crop up. For touring shows, this means focusing on ten major cities in North America, Europe, and Asia that we can visit annually—and hitting smaller cities every second or third year—while alternating a classic production like *Alegria* with a new show to avoid repetition.

Being more focused does not mean being less creative. To the contrary, we'll still be working with the best artists in the world and constantly exploring and developing lots of new ideas until we settle upon that one fantastic production that we love, that our partners can get excited about, and that ideally ends up running for decades. When I look back at my time at Cirque, we were the most successful whenever we operated this way.

Another way to look at this is that we are embracing what I would call "creative discipline." No matter what industry you are in, or what your professional goals are, the ability to focus, follow through, and get things done is at least as important as generating a million fantastic ideas. Yes, creativity does sometimes involve staring up at the stars and dreaming. But, as any musician, actor, dancer, poet, or painter can tell you, it also requires tremendous discipline. So does running a business.

GET LEAN

All that downtime during the pandemic gave us the chance to be disciplined in another way. We had the chance to review our corporate structure, reflect on what worked and what didn't, and look for inefficiencies and waste. We decided to leave the shows themselves alone—today, all casts and crews remain intact—but we looked hard for ways to reduce expenses elsewhere, to make our company more streamlined and agile. We thinned out bulky layers of management, scheduled Zoom meetings in lieu of expensive trips, and saved space by having people work from home at least part-time, even when it was safe to return to the office. Our highest priority remained the shows themselves because our casts and crews are the ones delivering the product to the consumers. Our rule: the further you are from the stage, the more economical your operation must be.

This weeding-out process is something any company can do anytime; there's no reason to wait for a global health emergency. Every year, during annual budget deliberations, review your whole operation carefully, as if you are starting from scratch. Look for efficiencies in areas furthest from your core business because that's where bloat tends to occur. After this rigorous accounting, we were pleased to end up with lower debt and in much better financial shape.

EMBRACE DIGITAL

The pandemic also changed our business for the better by opening our eyes to enormous opportunities in digital content. If anybody should have felt threatened by the rise of streaming services and online entertainment during the lockdown, it would be a live-entertainment company like ours. But we were surprised to find how much technology enhanced our brand, stoking consumer appetite for our live shows.

Less than two weeks after we shut down, we launched a free digital-content hub called CirqueConnect, accessible via the internet and social media channels, to stay in touch with our fans. Our first offering was a sixty-minute special featuring highlights from *Kurios: Cabinet of Curiosities*, *O*, and *Luzia*; a virtual-reality app; exercise videos and makeup tutorials; and soundtracks and music videos. Later, we added mini-documentaries on subjects like clowning, juggling, and acrobatics; reality shows featuring our performers; and more highlights from live events.

When we started testing this service, some of our staffers made a friendly wager of how large our audience would be. I was the most optimistic at two million views. That was way off. In those early tests, we got fourteen million views. At press time, we had gotten more than seventy million views. That's a dramatic illustration of the power of our brand, the value of our artistic content, and the huge potential for monetizing our online reach.

So many good things have emerged from CirqueConnect, which was put together by just two employees. It expanded our audience of younger, more digitally savvy fans. It helped to inspire MGM Studios (no connection to our Las Vegas partner MGM Resorts International) to greenlight a documentary about the reopening of *O*, directed by the award-winning filmmaker Dawn Porter. And it led to talks with various streaming platforms—Disney+, Amazon Prime Video, and Netflix, among others—about having us develop original artistic content for them.

The lesson, for me, is to keep an open mind about the tremendous power of digital, even in industries that perceive it as a threat: sectors like retail, manufacturing, or live events. Far from detracting from our live shows, reaching fans online improves our business by deepening our customers' level of engagement.

During the worst of the pandemic, audiences missed human contact so much that we are now experiencing an explosion of pent-up demand for our shows. Clearly, there is something in the human condition that craves physical connections with others, both onstage and in the audience. That's why, even pre-pandemic, shows in Las Vegas and Broadway had record-breaking years at the same time that streaming platforms were providing a glut of inexpensive entertainment. In the digital age, live shows have become special events that people are willing to pay a premium for, their value actually rising as online offerings become more plentiful.

On a fundamental level, audiences understand that what they see live—a concert, a comedy act, a magic show, a stage play, acrobatics—simply cannot be replicated digitally. Instead, they want online content that supplements their live experience: behind-the-scenes interviews, documentaries, soundtracks, show highlights. Our world has become a hybrid of both the physical and the digital, and companies that can meet the needs of consumers in both realms will ultimately be the most successful.

SPREAD THE GOSPEL OF CREATIVITY

Sometimes it's hard to remember what life was like before COVID-19. In early 2020, I was getting ready to retire. The company had been growing rapidly since being acquired by the TPG group, an IPO was being planned, and I was excited to be leaving on a high note.

All that was upended by the virus. After decades of success, I thought my career was ending in failure. Fortunately, I didn't have much time to dwell on that depressing thought. I was too focused on saving the company. During the worst of the crisis, I thought the most I could accomplish was to keep Cirque from going under and quietly pass the baton to the next CEO.

Then I met our new owners—including our cochairman of the board, Gabriel de Alba—who asked me to stay on to guide Cirque back to stability and profitability. After coming this far, how could I say no? As we began talking about relaunching our shows, I was inspired by the chance to help haul our ship up from the bottom of the sea and watch it sail away in glory, like a scene from our mystical water show, *O*.

Now that Cirque is back up and running, I realized that it is the perfect time to finally start the transition and let the next generation of leaders take over. As this book was going to press, I announced that our highly capable chief operations officer, Stéphane Lefebvre, would be taking the reins as chief executive officer. I will remain as full-time executive vice chairman of Cirque's board of directors for at least two years to help out with the transition any way I can. It makes me truly happy to know that our company will be in such good hands, and that it will be a very smooth transition.

After getting to know our new owners, I am more bullish on Cirque's future than ever before. It can be a challenge to understand how our unusual company works—it took me years to get the hang of it—so I was pleased that Gabriel spent two full weeks in Las Vegas during the reopening of *Mystère* and *O* to soak up our culture and learn the business, inside and out. (After all, he is our single largest shareholder, owning 30 percent of the company.) He saw rehearsals and shows, talked to cast and crew members, watched our interactions with MGM, and asked lots of questions. We also had time to develop genuine chemistry between the four members of our executive committee—Gabriel; his fellow cochairman, Jim Murren; Stéphane; and me—making me confident that whenever any issue arises, we will quickly resolve it.

As I reflect on my twenty years at Cirque, I am amazed at how much my outlook on life and business has changed. When I got that frantic phone call from Guy in late 2000, when he invited me to join his circus, I was living in another reality, one marked by caution, conformity, and stasis. Today, I feel liberated to help Stéphane and our board of directors pursue whatever strategies can best tap the creative power of our incredibly talented artists, employees, affiliates, and partners.

Though I have stepped back from day-to-day management, my goal is to continue being an evangelist for creativity in business, encouraging companies to throw off the old rules and restrictions of conventional thinking and unleash the creative spirit of their people. There is no time to waste. The great German poet Goethe put it beautifully, with a spirit we try to emulate in every Cirque du Soleil show: "Whatever you can do, or dream you can, begin it. Boldness has genius, power, and magic in it."

ACKNOWLEDGMENTS

———

So many people contributed to this book, and to my career at Cirque du Soleil, that it would be impossible to name them all. But here are a few:

Guy Laliberté, our founder, who taught me so much about the process of creativity and business. An amazing partner and friend, he built the company from scratch based on his own experiences as a street performer, a powerful legacy I have tried to propel forward.

My colleagues who were at my side in the trenches during the pandemic every step of the way: Stéphane Lefebvre, Jocelyn Côté, Diane Quinn, Eric Grilly, and Caroline Couillard.

My writing partner, Paul Keegan, who spent so much time with me and other sources while developing this project. He is not just a ghostwriter but a true collaborator who was totally engaged in the process from start to finish.

My agent, Evelyne Ouellet of Safira Entertainment, who books my speeches around the world and convinced me to write this book.

My literary agent, Mollie Glick of Creative Artists Agency, who gave me such wise editorial direction and found us a great publisher. This book never would have happened without her.

Our book team at HarperCollins, Matt Baugher and Sara Kendrick. Matt believed in this project from the beginning, flying to Montreal to visit me at Cirque and championing the book internally at the publisher. Sara offered many suggestions that made the book better and then improved it further still with her careful line editing.

François Colbert from Hautes Études Commerciales in Montréal, who asks me to speak to the students in his international program every year and pushed me to write this book.

My executive assistant, Rita Fiorante, who is so much more than her title suggests. She is a true colleague who read chapters, offered suggestions, and was always so kind and generous with her time.

Last but certainly not least, the thousands of artists and employees of Cirque du Soleil who demonstrate their commitment to deliver the best shows in the world with passion and dedication. None of the company's success would be possible without you—thank you!

INDEX

ABOUT THE AUTHOR

Daniel Lamarre is a French Canadian whose talent for leading creative companies became evident during his two decades at Cirque du Soleil. As chief executive officer, he guided the organization through a period of astounding growth and then brought it back to life during the massive upheaval of the COVID-19 pandemic. He is currently executive vice chairman of the company's board of directors.

When Daniel joined in 2001 as president of new ventures, Cirque du Soleil had two thousand employees and seven shows in performance. Five years later, he became chief executive, and the company grew to five thousand employees and forty-four shows around the world (including recent subsidiary acquisitions). At its peak, Cirque had annual sales of $1 billion, profit margins of twenty percent (EBITDA), and fifteen million people attending its shows per year, more than all thirty-nine Broadway shows combined.

Daniel's strengths include a laser-like focus during times of crisis and an ability to marry the needs of disparate groups and interests, finding positive solutions and outcomes for all— skills he fine-tuned throughout his long career. Before coming to Cirque, he was president and CEO of the TVA Group, Inc., Canada's largest television network. During his four years there, the Quebec-based company increased its market share by 40 percent and created LCN, the first French-language all-news network in North America.

Previously, Daniel was senior partner at National Public Relations, Inc., where, for more than a decade, he helped it grow from twenty employees in Montreal to become the largest public-relations company in Canada. His first major job came in 1981, at the age of twenty-eight, when he founded and directed the Montreal office of the world's largest PR firm, Burson-Marsteller.

In 2012, Daniel cofounded the C2 Montreal conference, a one-of-a-kind gathering of the world's creative and business elite. This platform for exploring innovative answers to commercial questions is consistent with his deeply held belief that without creativity, there *is* no commerce.

Daniel's outlook is resolutely international, but his roots are firmly in his tiny hometown of Grand-Mère, located in the French part of Canada. This strong sense of place and values is fundamental to how he does business and is also a source of great personal satisfaction. A natural storyteller, Daniel's best advice is usually delivered as a story from his rich personal experience. Drawing from his successes and failures, his weapons of choice are laughter and humility. His greatest joy is being the father of two grown children and grandfather of five lovely grandchildren. He enjoys a happy home life with his wife, the photographer Emmanuelle Duperre, and her two sons.

Daniel has been honored with doctorates from the Faculty of Law at McGill University; the University of Quebec in Trois-Rivières; and the Faculty of Arts at his alma mater, the University of Ottawa. Concerned about education and health-and-welfare issues, he supports a variety of charities. Daniel has been involved with Cirque du Monde, a worldwide social circus program that targets at-risk youth; the One Drop Foundation that Cirque founder Guy Laliberté created to provide healthy drinking water to underprivileged nations; and the Montreal Heart Institute Foundation, for which he serves as chairman of the board of directors.